Discovering Exodus

THE GUIDEPOSTS HOME BIBLE STUDY PROGRAM

Floyd W. Thatcher   *General Editor*
Robin White Goode   *Associate Editor*
Bob E. Patterson   *Technical Consultant*

The Book of Exodus

Discovering Exodus   R. Scott Walker
What This Scripture Means to Me   Evelyn Bence
Cover Artist   Ben Wohlberg
Map   Janice Gibson

DISCOVERING EXODUS

The Guideposts Home Bible Study Program

GUIDEPOSTS®

Carmel   New York   10512

The photographs on the pages below are reproduced with the permission of the following photographers:

D.H. Condit: 15 *(top and bottom),* 21 *(bottom),* 49 *(top and bottom),* 72
Bruce Cresson: 21 *(top),* 95, 142, 160
William LaSor: 28, 111

Quotation on p. 163 from *The Summer of the Great Grandmother* by Madeleine L'Engle used by permission. Farrar, Straus and Giroux, publishers.

THE GUIDEPOSTS HOME BIBLE STUDY PROGRAM
The Book of Exodus
    1. DISCOVERING EXODUS
    2. My Working Bible
    3. Knowing More About Exodus

Contents

Publisher's Introduction

The biblical drama intensifies as we move into this study of Exodus, the sequel to the Book of Genesis. The Genesis narrative ended with the sons of Jacob—the Hebrews—comfortably settled in Egypt's Nile Delta, the Land of Goshen. Joseph died soon thereafter.

The Exodus narrative opens with the descendants of Jacob and his sons still living in Goshen, but the circumstances had changed drastically. No longer were they welcome legal aliens—now they were slaves most likely providing the physical labor needed in the building of public structures which can still be seen, if only in ruins, in Egypt today.

The Hebrew title for this book is *shemoth*—"Names," taken from the opening words of the book, "these are the *names.*" However, the Hellenistic Jews who translated the Hebrew Scriptures into Alexandrian Greek sometime between 250 and 100 B.C. labeled the book "Exodus" after its central event—the "going out" of the Hebrews from Egyptian bondage.

As in the Book of Genesis, the central Person in the Book of Exodus is God—"Yahweh" to the Hebrews. Throughout these eight lessons we will grasp for ourselves the primary theme that threads its way throughout the entire narrative—God is revealing

Himself, making Himself known, to His people. He made Himself known to Moses at the "burning bush." He made Himself known to the "sons of Jacob" through Moses during their final days in Egypt. He made Himself known to the Egyptian people through the drama of the ten plagues. He then continued making Himself known to the Hebrew people as He supplied their needs and led them across the desert wilderness to Mount Sinai. And it is there that He made Himself known through the reaffirmation of the covenant and the giving of the Ten Commandments.

The central human character in the Exodus narrative is Moses—the very human, yet God-directed man, who through unique circumstances was raised as the stepson of an Egyptian princess in Pharaoh's court. Yet, we discover, he did not forget his roots, and at the age of eighty Moses led his people under God's direction out of slavery to Mount Sinai and ultimately to the borders of the Land of Promise.

We also see in the Exodus drama the birth of a nation, as the descendants of Abraham, Isaac, and Jacob are transformed from an unruly and complaining group of former slaves into a nation equal to the task of occupying Canaan. The Exodus Event became the central tenet of the Hebrew religion. And for the Christian, an understanding of what is found in these studies is of paramount importance in grasping the meaning of so much of our New Testament faith.

As we will discover in the events and message of the Book of Exodus, our God is not a distant deity who remains aloof from His people. To the Hebrews, He "dwelt among them," and to the Christian, He lives within us. Our God does not leave us to find our own way in the twentieth-century wilderness—instead He is leading us just as surely as He led our spiritual ancestors in the cloud by day and in the pillar of fire by night.

Our present day adventure of faith comes alive with new meaning as we walk in the sandals of Moses and the Hebrew people. Their longings and their dreams were not that much different from ours. From them and their story we catch a fresh vision of a God who cares and is with us.

Preface

To truly understand the drama of Exodus we must first see this ancient saga from the perspective of its importance within the broad vista of the entire Bible. Though the Book of Exodus can stand alone, it gains its deepest meaning in relational unity with all of the books of the Bible.

Above all else, the Bible is a record of how God has, since the beginning of time, yearned and struggled to reveal Himself to men and women, and to live in spiritual relationship with them. God's attempt to reveal or disclose Himself to people is depicted in the Bible in three stages.

First, He revealed Himself to the human race through the act of creation. But when sin entered the world and people attempted to be like God, the results were tragic. And while throughout the centuries there were a few who remained faithful to the true God, the majority, it seemed, turned to false gods.

Next, God revealed Himself through the life and history of the nation of Israel. It began with Abraham when he left northern Mesopotamia around 1850 B.C. and migrated to Canaan. In responding to God's call and leading, Abraham became the father of what was to become the nation of Israel.

God's covenant promise continued on with the Patriarchs—Isaac and Jacob. It was with the life of Jacob's young son, Joseph, that the lights began to glow dimly on the stage of the Book of Exodus. Due to sibling rivalry and jealousy, Joseph was sold by his brothers to slave traders who took the young boy to Egypt where he was resold into slavery. Over time and through intriguing events, Joseph was freed from slavery and rose to become a powerful government official.

It was around 1700 B.C. that a famine devastated Canaan and Joseph's brothers traveled to Egypt for food supplies. And it was there they ultimately came to realize that the official from whom they were obtaining food was their long lost brother. Amends were made, and the entire Jacob clan migrated from Canaan to the rich delta of Egypt.

Over the next five hundred years the descendants of Jacob—the Hebrews—became a significant minority population in Egypt. But when a new Pharaoh came to power who "knew not Joseph," the Hebrews became slaves and were subjected to cruel tyranny.

It was then that God set events into motion that would free His "chosen" people. The account of their rescue and deliverance makes the story line for the Book of Exodus.

The primary theme in the Book of Exodus is that God provides for the needs of His people. In these eight lessons God's constant provision for the needs of His people will be seen from eight perspectives:

1. God Provides Leadership for His People—Chapters 1 through 4.

2. God Provides Freedom for His People—Chapters 5 through 12.

3. God Provides Welfare for His People—Chapters 13 through 18.

4. God Provides Laws for His People—Chapters 19 through 24.

5. God Provides Worship for His People—Chapters 25 through 31.

6. God Provides Forgiveness for His People—Chapter 32.

7. God Provides His Presence for His People—Chapters 33 and 34.

8. God Provides Direction for His People—Chapters 36 through 40.

In Exodus we have the story of how God is faithful to undergird and support those who struggle—and fail—and struggle again to live in personal relationship with God and follow His guidance in their lives.

We would probably not be wrong to say that the Hebrew people were liberated by God sometime in the middle decades of 1200 B.C.; and ultimately they reached their Promised Land. As they became a nation, they struggled for over twelve hundred years to live in obedient relationship with God and reveal Him to the rest of the world. But their constant disobedience and "hardness of heart" prevented them from fulfilling God's purpose for them and for His world.

At what seemed their lowest point, God entered human history in the person of Jesus Christ, the ultimate revelation of who He is. In the gift of Jesus for the salvation of humankind we see the theme of the ancient Book of Exodus fulfilled—God does provide for the needs of His people!

As in the Exodus story, our needs are often met in surprising and unsuspecting ways. But of this we can be sure: God is faithful to respond to and support everyone who comes to Him. And God's intense and eternal desire to live in relationship with His people will not be thwarted!

Among the most ancient of traditions is that Moses was the author of the Book of Exodus. But scholars readily agree for the most part that the authorship question is exceptionally complex. Undoubtedly, it is the work of several writers. Authorship is not a particular concern of ours in this study—it is the message that is of primary importance.

For the Christian, the Book of Exodus is of primary importance in understanding both our faith and the New Testament. While God is the central character in the drama of the Exodus, it is the towering figure of Moses that dominates the human scene. The events in which he figured—delivery from Egypt, the Passover, the provision of food in the desert, the giving of the Law on Mount Sinai, the building of the

Tabernacle, and the establishment of the priesthood—are central not only to the Exodus story but to our Judeo-Christian heritage. The New Testament contains forty-four quotations from the Book of Exodus.

Now, let us move back across this particular stage of human history and begin our journey with God's people, the Hebrews, as we discover with them that God does truly provide for the needs of His people.

LESSON 1
Exodus 1–4

God Provides Leadership for His People

Lord God, Thank You for leading me—even when the road seems rocky and the way dark, I know by faith that You are making my paths straight. AMEN.

One of the most convincing and persuasive things about the Bible is that its story grows out of events and finds its solid ring of authenticity because it is rooted in history. For this reason, we can better understand the Exodus story as we become familiar with its setting and background.

Approximately two thousand years before the birth of Jesus, Egypt was a major world power and a cultural center that attracted tribal and nomadic people from all over the ancient world. Around 1900 B.C. there was a particularly strong influx of Semitic people into Egypt to escape a drought. From within this immigrant mass, a revolutionary coalition formed and, aided by some disgruntled Egyptians, overthrew the government around 1720 B.C. The new rulers of Egypt were called the Hyksos—"rulers of foreign lands."

It was during this time that Joseph probably arrived in Egypt as a slave. Then a few years later Joseph's father and his entire clan settled in the east-

The Birth of Moses (1:1–2:10)
Living in a State of In-between

13

ern Nile Delta in Goshen. These events occurred in all probability between 1700 and 1650 B.C.

It is quite likely that Joseph's meteoric rise in government and the warm welcome given to Jacob's clan can be attributed to the presence of the Semitic Hyksos Pharaohs. However, in 1550 B.C. the Hyksos rulers were overthrown by Amenotep I and control of the throne of the Pharaohs was regained by native Egyptians. It was at this time that minority groups like the Hebrews began to lose both privilege and security.

Modern scholars are quite generally agreed that the Pharaoh of the Hebrews' darkest hour of oppression was Ramses II. He reigned over Egypt a total of sixty-seven years—1290–1224 B.C. Master builder that he was, Ramses II built a series of forts along the eastern border of Goshen and built the northern capital of his empire, the city of Ramses and the adjacent storage city of Pithom—both in the northeastern Nile Delta. His amazing building achievements were made possible by conscripted slave labor which included the Hebrews. The mummy of Ramses II can be seen in the museum at Cairo.

As the Exodus story begins, the Hebrews are suffering under the bondage of cruel and oppressive slavery. Even though part of their four-hundred-year stay in Egypt had been spent under oppression, the Exodus writer says, "And the children of Israel were fruitful, and increased abundantly, and multiplied, and waxed exceedingly mighty; and the land was filled with them" (1:7). Despite adversity and oppression, their numbers had increased.

It is not by accident that the writer of Exodus begins his story by stressing the growth of the Hebrew people. In effect, he is looking back nearly six hundred years to the promise that God made to Abraham when He brought him out into the night and said, "Look now toward heaven, and tell the stars, if thou be able to number them. . . . So shall thy seed be" (Gen. 15:5). A generation later God made the same promise to Isaac (Gen. 26:2–5), and then again to his son Jacob (Gen. 35:11–12). The Exodus writer began his story by underscoring the fact that God had moved steadily down the years of history

The Great Sphinx of Gizeh located near the Pyramid of Khafra. The sphinx was a mythical beast of ancient Egypt that symbolized the pharaoh in his divine role as the sun god Ra. As a rule the sphinx had the head of a man and the body of a lion.

The Temple of Isis built by Queen Hatsepshut. Isis was the nature goddess of ancient Egypt. This temple was approximately two hundred years old when Moses was born.

fulfilling His promise. Most certainly, the descendants of Abraham had "multiplied" by the time of our Exodus story.

However, the promise made to Abraham hadn't been completely fulfilled. For God also said, "I will make of thee a great nation. . . . Unto thy seed [descendants] will I give this land" (Gen. 12:2, 7). Even though the Hebrews had grown in numbers, they were not yet a nation nor had they received and occupied their land. God's promise was still in the creative process of becoming reality. And so, probably without intending to do so, the writer of Exodus is laying the foundation for a spiritual truth that will be developed throughout his entire story: those who choose to follow God must be willing to live in a "state of in-between."

Now, what do I mean by a "state of in-between"? Quite simply, Christians must see that God works over the course of centuries to bring His promises to fulfillment. In speaking of time, the Psalmist writes that the seemingly long years of our life are really very short—the length of a hand when viewed from God's eternal perspective (Psa. 39:5). The writer of 2 Peter echoes the same idea as he quotes from another psalm (90:4), "One day is with the Lord as a thousand years, and a thousand years as one day" (2 Peter 3:8). Naturally, it is impossible for us in our humanness and impatience to view time as God does. But we must be willing to "wait on the Lord" and be willing also to live in a "state of in-between."

When I was a child in the third grade, my science teacher explained to our class how a potato could be planted in the earth and the "eyes" would sprout and grow new potatoes. She then gave us some cuttings to take home and plant.

With great excitement I planted my cuttings in a corner of my mother's flower garden. But several days later when I couldn't see any sprouts creeping above ground, I began to grow impatient and doubt my teacher's word. At the end of the first full week, I decided to dig up the cuttings to see if they were growing. Sure enough, they were—slowly! However, I had almost destroyed the growth process in my childish quest for reassurance.

Impatience is a stressful factor in the life of us all. The agony of waiting is a pain we endure only with great difficulty. And yet to be a Christian we must be patient. If we grow fretful and restless and begin to "dig up the patch," looking for constant reassurance, we will only grow despondent, exhausted, and weary.

Instead, if we rise high enough above our everyday problems to see the broad vista of history unfold before us, we can be assured that God is at work, even though we live in a slow-moving "state of in-between."

In the sixth century B.C., we find that the author of Isaiah 40:31 and many of his fellow Jews were living in exile in Babylonia. Some of them had spent their entire lives waiting to return to Jerusalem and had died with their dreams unfulfilled. Many had grown impatient and despairing. Others felt that God had forgotten them. But to this weary and restless people Isaiah spoke these immortal words, "But they that wait upon the Lord shall renew their strength; they shall mount up with wings as eagles; they shall run, and not be weary; and they shall walk, and not faint" (Isa. 40:31). Isaiah had learned one of the most important lessons of history. True faith is the ability to "wait upon the Lord."

When we find ourselves in our own muddy potato patch ready to abandon all hope and frantically dig up our lives, roots and all, we must remember the example of the Hebrews. Both Moses and Isaiah "waited upon the Lord." And because they waited, they were able to mount up with wings like eagles; to run, and not be weary; to walk and not faint. And so can you and I!

Building Blocks of Greatness

While the Hebrews didn't know it at the time, God was very much aware of their oppression and suffering—the stage was being set for Moses, who in God's time, would lead them to freedom. From our point in Christian history we see a similar movement of events in the coming of Jesus. Again and again, we see God accomplishing His eternal purpose through people. In the words of Saint Francis of Asissi, we are God's "instruments of peace."

However, though we are to be instruments of peace, God's anointed leader, Moses, was born into a situation that was anything but peaceful. As the Hebrew population began to expand and grow in the region of Goshen, Pharaoh began to feel increasingly threatened. He remembered well the Hyksos who overthrew his forefathers. And he decided to make sure that such a group of foreigners would never be allowed to become a political force again. So he set a strategy in motion that would smother the idea of revolution (1:10).

In order to weaken the Hebrews, Pharaoh ordered their midwives to kill all male babies born to Hebrew women (1:16). However, when the midwives did not comply with his wishes, Pharaoh publicly proclaimed that every son born to Hebrew women must be thrown into the Nile river (1:22). Under such a reign of genocide and terror was Moses born.

Who was Moses? Outside of biblical sources, nothing is known about this leader of the Hebrews. He is mentioned in no Egyptian document, nor in any other surviving archives of the ancient Near East. However, Moses is repeatedly referred to in the pages of the Old and New Testaments, and is venerated today by Christians, Jews, and Muslims. There can be little doubt of his historical existence.

As to Moses' family, in the opening chapters of Exodus we are simply told that "a man of the house of Levi . . . took to wife a daughter of Levi. And the woman conceived, and bare a son" (2:1–2). Into such trackless anonymity was Moses born. However, we later discover that Moses' father was named Amram and that he was married to his father's sister, Jochobed (6:20), an acceptable custom at that time in the Near East. Also, we are told that Moses had an older brother, Aaron (6:20), and a sister, Miriam (15:20).

With the birth of Moses we can see that so often the creative Spirit of God uses unknown people to be the building blocks of greatness. For example, who was Abram? A nameless face lost in the antiquity of Sumer-Chaldea. Who was Moses? A son of Hebrew slaves whose names are recorded in Exodus almost as an afterthought. Who was Jesus Christ? The son of

Mary, a peasant girl, probably so poor as to not even be able to slip an innkeeper enough money "to make room" for the birth of a baby. It seems that just as God created the world from nothingness, so He touches the lives of unknown people who think they are "nothing" and transforms them into men and women of tremendous leadership capability.

Many people have often seen the shadow of Moses loom over the figure of Martin Luther King, Jr. Like Moses, King was not perfect. He had his human frailties. Like Moses, King found himself in the midst of his kinfolk who were oppressed by a social system. And like Moses, Martin Luther King began his life as a nobody—the son of a black Baptist minister quietly tucked away in the backstreets of Atlanta, Georgia.

However, in the hands of God a nobody became a somebody. A little black boy grew up to become a man who, in the providence of God, gained the ear of presidents, the attention of millions, and shook the social conscience of a nation. Though a sniper's bullet fired in hate did in time kill this man, it could not dull his prophetic vision and the unfolding of his dream. God had transformed Martin Luther King into an "instrument of His peace."

Perhaps God's greatest frustration in His ongoing creative process is that too many people do not have a vision for who they can be when touched by His creative hand. God's power is limited only by our misconception that we are anonymous, unimportant people, lost in a crowd with little to offer anyone. We must remember that God always creates building blocks of greatness out of "nothing."

When Moses was born, his mother refused to obey Pharaoh and murder her son. Risking her life, she hid the baby for three months (2:2). Then, for reasons unexplained, she decided she could keep her baby no longer and devised a plan to save his life. It was a calculated risk, but one which, in the plan of God, worked beautifully.

Very craftily, Moses' mother took a wicker basket and waterproofed it by covering it with tar and pitch. She then put the child in the basket and set it in

Jochobed's Cunning Plan

shallow water among the papyrus reeds along the bank of the Nile. Jochobed purposely hid the basket by a section of the riverbank frequently used by the royal Egyptian family for bathing. Then she stationed Moses' sister to watch the basket from a distance and see if it was discovered (2:3–5).

As was planned, the baby was discovered—by none other than Pharaoh's daughter. Her maternal instincts and feminine sensitivity instantly bonded her to the abandoned little boy and she felt deep compassion and empathy. Even though she clearly recognized that the baby was a Hebrew (2:6), she decided to save his life.

It is interesting that the Hebrew word for basket used by the writer of Exodus is found in only one other place in the entire Bible. And, that other reference is to Noah's ark, another floating vessel made waterproof by tar and pitch. It seems likely that the writer of Exodus is subtly, perhaps intentionally, connecting the story of Noah to the story of Moses and is underscoring the theme of how God twice saved men from drowning so they might in turn save God's people. Noah's life was spared by the ark so that he might replenish the human race. And Moses was kept alive by means of a floating basket so that he might lead God's chosen people to freedom.

During the first tumultuous centuries of the spread of Christianity, the church was often depicted symbolically as an ark, on the walls of the Roman catacombs, in frescoes, and within paintings. From the beginning, it has been recognized that it is the warm fellowship and bolstering relationships of fellow Christians within the church that keep us afloat and alive when our world grows stormy and threatening. It seems that a loving God always provides a conveyance—an ark, a basket, or a church—to protect His people from the dangers of life. In days of turmoil these shelters often seem brittle, unstable, and inadequate. But God keeps His people safe so that they in turn can survive to lead others toward the promised land of salvation through Jesus Christ.

The Naming of a Future Leader

As soon as Pharaoh's daughter discovered the baby, Moses' sister appeared and asked, "Shall I go

Two views of the Nile River, the lifeline of Egypt. Except for the Nile, Egypt would have been one massive desert. But as long ago as 4,000 B.C. irrigation systems were established that made possible lush harvests.

and call to thee a nurse of the Hebrew women, that she may nurse the child for thee?" (2:7). Pharaoh's daughter consented and Moses' mother was immediately summoned to the scene. She was then instructed to take the baby home and nurse him until he was weaned, a process that normally lasted three years according to Hebrew custom.

When the child was weaned, Jochobed took him back to Pharaoh's daughter and "he became her son" (2:10). It was then that he was named Moses because, as she said, "I drew him out of the water."

The name of Moses has caused much discussion among Old Testament scholars. It is Egyptian in origin and can mean either "to give birth," "son," or something like "seed of the water." The name usually appears in shortened form in Egyptian names like Thutmose.

However, the author of Exodus associates the name of Moses and the name's history not with an Egyptian word, but rather a Hebrew verb sounding much like Moses. This verb means "he who is drawn out (of the Nile)" or "he who draws forth." Clearly the writer of Exodus saw in the naming of Moses that from his infancy, he was to be the one who "drew forth" his people from the oppression of slavery just as he was also "drawn forth" from certain death in the Nile.

In the naming of Moses, we see a major theme in Exodus announced that "God provides leadership for His people." Throughout history, God has continually touched the lives of people and enabled them to "draw forth" others from all types of bondage and enslavement.

When Jesus began His public ministry and returned for the first time to His hometown synagogue in Nazareth, He announced that He would be one who would "draw forth" others from the bondage of sin. He did so by publicly reading from Isaiah 61:1–2 and then applying these words to Himself, "The Spirit of the Lord is upon me, because he hath anointed me to preach the gospel to the poor; he hath sent me to heal the broken hearted, to preach deliverance to the captives, and recovering of sight to the blind, to set at liberty them that are bruised, to preach the acceptable year of the Lord" (Luke 4:18–19). Upon reading these words, Jesus then said, "This day is this scripture fulfilled in your ears" (Luke 4:21).

As Christians, we are called to be people who "draw forth" others from all forms of bondage. And in this service to others, we paradoxically find our greatest freedom. Phillips Brooks, a prominent American Episcopal clergyman, once said, "No man in this world attains to freedom from slavery except by entrance into some higher servitude."

As with Moses, we begin the process of becoming free when we assume the responsibility of being people who "draw forth" others from physical, spiritual, and social bondage. For true freedom begins in the acceptance of the servant's role. The greatest leaders throughout history have not been lords and power-brokers but rather servants of the people. They have been those who "draw forth."

On the night that Jesus shared His final meal with His disciples, we are told that following the meal He put on the meager dress of a servant and went around and washed His disciples' feet. It is interesting that under Jewish law not even a slave could be compelled to wash another person's feet. And yet, Jesus had the humility to stoop and wash His disciples' feet.

Besides demonstrating His love for them, Jesus wanted to show them that nobody is above serving another. With words that have echoed through the centuries He said, "For I have given you an example, that ye should do as I have done to you. Verily, verily, I say unto you, The servant is not greater than his lord; neither he that is sent greater than he that sent him. If ye know these things, happy are ye if ye do them" (John 13:15–17). Jesus, the Lord of all, was servant to all. And because He was willing to serve others, indeed, even to die for others, He was one who "drew forth" others from spiritual enslavement to freedom.

In the city of Charleston, where I live, we have a very unusual police chief. Frequently we see him directing traffic instead of sitting behind a desk. Often he will walk a beat or respond to an emergency. The policemen of our city know that their chief is not "too good" to work with them and, as a result, he is gaining national notoriety as one of the best law enforcement officials in the country.

However, what has impressed me most about our police chief is his attitude of service. A devout Jew, he often talks with teenagers about the dangers of drugs. Being a black man, he is well aware of the evil of racial prejudice and tactfully works to remove it. His religious faith has led him to be a servant to all and a man who seeks to liberate the people of our city from the bondage of drug traffic, criminal behavior, pornography, and other social evils that attack and degrade our lives. This man has been called out by his convictions to serve others. He has found that leadership is rooted in servanthood.

From Pharaoh's Court to Midian (2:11–2:25)
A Flame Is Lit

As in the life of Jesus Christ, there is a sudden leap in the biographical narrative from Moses' birth to manhood (2:11). The Old Testament tells us nothing about Moses' childhood or adolescence. Josephus, the Jewish historian writing in the first century A.D., states that in his youth Moses led an Egyptian army against Ethiopia, captured their capital, and married the defeated king's daughter. However, this is most likely a myth and cannot be further substantiated. For his purposes, it is apparent that the writer of Exodus saw little need to include in his account episodes from Moses' childhood.

When the spotlight shines again on Moses, we find a young man in great struggle with his self-identity. From all outward appearances, he was an Egyptian of royal blood. Quite likely he had received a fine education (Acts 7:22) and lived in regal splendor. It is thought by many authorities that Moses was well educated in Egypt's temple schools and was trained as a scribe. But inwardly Moses knew that he was a Hebrew and the oppression of his people was a great concern to him.

In Exodus 2:11, we read that Moses "went out unto his brethren, and looked on their burdens." Obviously, Moses was having difficulty turning his back on the abuse and enslavement of his fellow Israelites. So when Moses saw an Egyptian taskmaster brutally beating a Hebrew slave, something snapped and a flame was lit. He attacked the Egyptian and, in his anger and pent up frustration, killed him and hid the body in the sand (2:12).

The writer of Exodus doesn't moralize on Moses' act of violence. He doesn't praise or condemn it. What is clear, though, is that people used by God in the Old Testament are often very earthy, volatile, lustful, and sinful human beings like you and me.

For example, Jacob maliciously and deceitfully tricked his own brother, Esau, and stole his legal birthright. Here we see Moses murdering a man in a fit of rage. David committed adultery with his general's wife and then had him purposely killed in battle to hide his sin with Bathsheba. All of these leaders of the Hebrew people were human, sinful, and morally frail.

But this doesn't mean that a righteous God overlooks sin or condones our human weaknesses. It does say, though, that God's leaders are not immune to mistakes, bad judgment, and grave error. What we learn from Moses and countless others in the Bible story is that a sinful act, though costly and unjustified, does not necessarily need to ruin our lives nor cause us to lose our effectiveness as witnesses to others. Rather, as Jesus told the woman who had been caught in adultery, we must "go, and sin no more" (John 8:11).

The New Testament is clear that God is always ready to forgive us and use us despite our sinfulness. But at the same time He intends for us to learn from our sins.

A Stinging Rejection

Upon murdering the Egyptian, Moses hid his body in the sand only to discover the next day that his act of violence had been uncovered (2:13). While Moses was intervening in a fight between two Hebrews, one of them responded to his efforts with wrathful impudence, "Who made thee a prince and a judge over us? intendest thou to kill me, as thou killedst the Egyptian?" (2:14). Stung by this retort, Moses realized that his murderous act of the previous day was a secret no longer.

At the same time Moses was becoming aware of

some other things about himself. Behind his identity crisis and his attack on the Egyptian taskmaster was emerging a clear and pressing desire for justice and the liberation of the enslaved. The flames of righteous indignation against injustice were being kindled into a blazing fire. Moses was being melted, hammered, and shaped into a leadership role over the fires of an ethical cause—human freedom and the enslavement of the human spirit.

However, in the Hebrew slave's retort to Moses, another theme is sounded. Even though Moses is recognized as a Hebrew and he is trying to keep two of his countrymen from fighting among themselves, he is rejected by his own people with the caustic comment: Who made you a prince or a judge over us? While he didn't know it at the time, for the rest of his life, Moses would confront the thankless task, which all leaders face, of trying to help people who will inevitably respond by being critical, rebellious, and headstrong.

The Escape to Midian

When Pharaoh learned that Moses had killed an Egyptian, we read that "he sought to slay Moses" (2:15). But Moses ran for his life to the land of Midian, an arid region east of Egypt. It lay on the eastern shore of the Gulf of Aqaba, to the south of Palestine. The Midianites were distant cousins of the Hebrews because their forefather, Midian, was the son of Abraham and his second wife, Keturah (Gen. 25:2). Ironically, it was Midianite traders who, centuries earlier, had sold Joseph into slavery in Egypt.

The Drama at the Well

Our writer next tells us that when Moses, now a refugee, arrived at a certain place in Midian, "he sat down by a well" (2:15)—the traditional meeting place in the Near East at that time. While resting and waiting there, he observed this scenario. Seven sisters, daughters of "the priest of Midian," arrived to draw water for their flocks. But no sooner had they arrived than some roughneck shepherds also appeared on the scene and tried to drive the girls away. But Moses, undoubtedly an imposing figure, rose to the defense of the seven sisters "and watered their flock" (2:17).

Later, when the sisters arrived home, their father, Reuel, expressed surprise that they had finished watering the herd so quickly. They told him they'd had help from an Egyptian in watering their flock and that he had also driven off the shepherds who had harassed them. Then, typical of the warm hospitality characteristic of the nomadic people of the ancient Near East, their father insisted that they return to the well and bring the stranger to their camp "that he may eat bread" (2:18–20).

It is then, without giving any details, that the Exodus writer tells us that Moses settled down to live with this priest and respected chieftain of Midian who is referred to in our story as both Reuel and Jethro (2:18, 3:1). The Midianites, like the Hebrews, were nomadic shepherds, but the Kenite group to which Jethro and his family belonged were also craftsmen in metal. They were an intelligent and sophisticated people.

Reminiscent of the Jacob and Laban story, we are next told that Moses went to work for Jethro and married Zipporah, the chieftain's daughter. Then, telescoped into a few words, we learn that Moses and Zipporah had a son and named him Gershom, which meant "a sojourner in a foreign land."

Moses Finds a New Home

In many ways Moses' years in Midian as a shepherd and member of Jethro's clan was a "time-out" period—probably a time of reflection, a time of quiet and maturing. Most certainly he didn't know what was ahead.

As Christians, we, too, need our "time-out" periods even though we find it much more exciting to live in the intensity of "our Egypt." But we also need our times "in the desert"—times of quiet, away from the busy hurly-burly of life. The Psalmist apparently had this in mind when he wrote about lying "down in green pastures" so our souls would be restored in preparation for future times of service (Psa. 23).

I recall so well when I graduated from college I hadn't made up my mind just what vocational route

Life's Time-Out Periods

27

It was in a setting something like pictured above Moses spent some forty years working as a shepherd for his father-in-law.

I would take. Options I was considering were law, government service, the Christian ministry, but I was having difficulty making a decision. During those days of indecision I felt very much like I was stuck out in the desert and was wandering around in circles, fearful that life would pass me by.

Fortunately, in the midst of my quandary, I was offered a job singing with a Christian music group that was touring college campuses. Though I was overjoyed and quickly accepted this exciting and novel opportunity, I was still haunted by the idea that I might be wasting valuable time. Uneasily, I watched many of my graduating classmates enter law school, business school, and other more traditional vocational paths.

And yet, as I traveled to college campuses over the next twelve months and interacted with students, it became clear that God was leading me into the Christian ministry. My experiences were becoming catalysts for decision-making. What I had feared might be a possible waste of time turned into one of the most formative periods of my life.

God Responds

We come now in our lesson to a brief parenthesis. We're told that "it came to pass in process of time, that the king of Egypt died: and the children of Israel sighed by reason of the bondage, and they cried, and their cry came up unto God by reason of the bondage" (2:23). It seems likely here, although there is a difference of opinion among scholars, that the reference is to the death of Seti I, the founder of the nineteenth dynasty, and the assuming of the throne by his son, Ramses II. The point being made is that there was no change in the plight of the Hebrews by the shift in power. The new Pharaoh carried on the stern and brutal policies of his father.

This was indeed a time of acute crisis for the Hebrews—the sons of Jacob. And now something very significant happens in the story. Up to this time the writer has not made a direct reference to God, but, in response to the Hebrews' prayer for help, God moves to center stage in the story of His people. We read, "And God heard their groaning, and God remembered his covenant with Abraham, with Isaac, and with Jacob. And God looked upon the children of Israel, and God had respect unto them [God was aware of their dire situation and felt deep concern for them]" (2:24–25).

With these words, the drama shifts from past-tense reflections on the early years of Moses to present tense; as we participate in the story and witness God's power being unleashed to free His people from bondage. From here on, the Exodus story begins to gain momentum. The introductions are over!

Called to Leadership (3:1–4:31)
A Marvelous Sight

We come back now to Moses in the desert as we read, "Now Moses kept the flock of Jethro his father in law, the priest of Midian: and he led the flock to the backside [west side] of the desert, and came to the mountain of God, even to Horeb" (3:1). It is quite likely that Moses frequently had to roam over a wide expanse of desert wilderness in order to find forage for his sheep.

The names Mount Horeb and Mount Sinai are synonymous and are used interchangeably in the Exodus story. Though its location has long been open to debate, "the mountain of God" has traditionally been positioned in the southeastern area of the Sinai peninsula. There is considerable agreement, however, that the biblical Horeb or Sinai is what is known today as Jebel Musa, a peak that stretches skyward 7,449 feet. Here, while tending the sheep on the foothills of Horeb, Moses had a deeply spiritual and unforgettable encounter. As he trudged along on this particular day, his eyes suddenly became riveted on a bush that was burning in the distance. The sight of a bush burning wasn't especially unusual, because the intense heat in the desert often caused a dry and brittle bush to explode into flame. But this was different. For as Moses watched, he saw that "the bush was not consumed" (3:2) by the flames.

As the storyteller unravels the scene, we can almost hear Moses mutter to himself, "I will now turn aside, and see this great [strange] sight, why the bush is not burnt" (3:3). Moses' curiosity drew him in the direction of that burning bush as if he were being pulled by a giant magnet.

Curiosity and action were the right responses. For "when the Lord saw that he [Moses] turned aside to see, God called unto him out of the midst of the bush, and said, Moses, Moses. And he said, Here am I. And he [God] said, Draw not nigh hither [don't come any closer]: put off thy shoes from off thy feet, for the place whereon thou standest is holy ground. Moreover he said, I am the God of thy father, the God of Abraham, the God of Isaac, and the God of Jacob. And Moses hid his face; for he was afraid to look upon God" (3:4–6).

I have quoted this entire first part of what God said to Moses because of the high drama in the scene. A burning bush that wasn't reduced to ashes was a strange and awesome sight that could only be topped by a voice penetrating the desert silence that says, "Moses . . . I am the God of thy father." At that point we can be sure that God had Moses' attention!

But let's stop and reflect for a moment and ask, "What would have happened if when Moses saw that bush burning in the distance, he had just shrugged his shoulders and walked on by?"

From our vantage point some three thousand years later, the answer is obvious: he would have lost out on a dramatic encounter with God. Had the action gone that way, we would be very critical. But at the same time we have to wonder just how often God has put a "burning bush" on our horizon and we have failed to "turn aside" to see "this great sight."

How often do we have opportunities for God to communicate with us out of even the common occurrences in our lives, and yet we miss out in our mad rush to reach our "mountaintop"? Yet, if we would just slow down—if we would look at that sunset, wrap that little child in our arms, stand for a moment in the rain, or meditate on the twinkling star, we, too, might come to see that we walk every day on holy ground.

Our God is One who longs to make us aware that He is a burning Presence, and, with Moses, we must "turn aside, and see" a God who will challenge us to a life of serving others. At the same time, though, our God is humble enough to speak to us out of the ordinary, everyday occurrence—even a wilted bush. Our task is to be vigilant and listen.

The God Who "Comes Down"

But God wasn't through. Next He told Moses that He was aware of the suffering of the Hebrew people, for He adds, "I am come down to deliver them out of the hand of the Egyptians" (3:8).

It is true that Moses lived in a prescientific age when primitive people literally believed that the gods lived on the rim of the clouds or on the summit of mountains. So, in one sense, it wouldn't have been surprising for Moses to hear God saying "I will come down." This idea would have fit comfortably within his ancient understanding of the universe. However, what was really startling to Moses was that this God, speaking from the bush, was saying that He was taking the initiative and coming down—to draw closer—to people!

One of the characteristics of the ancient Canaanite and Egyptian gods was that they were perceived as being distant and removed from people. While it was thought that the gods could be crudely manipulated into responding to peoples' needs, it was believed they really didn't care about the plight of ordinary humans. Indeed, the ancient Greeks used to describe their gods by an adjective from which we derive our modern English word "apathy." They believed their gods were apathetic toward the concerns and needs of people.

Yet, Moses now heard that the God of his fathers was not apathetic. Rather, He was "coming down" because He had "seen the afflictions" of His people. This God of the burning bush would not only free His people, He would "bring them up out of that land [Egypt] unto a good land and a large, unto a land flowing with milk and honey" (3:8).

The Good News that thunders across the pages of the Old Testament and finds its fulfillment in the New Testament is that our God is not apathetic. This God who spoke from a burning bush to Moses and later was revealed in Jesus Christ takes the initiative to "come down" and free us from all kinds of bondage.

"Who am I?"

As God continued, it became clear that Moses was being given a special assignment, "Come now therefore, and I will send thee unto Pharaoh, that thou mayest bring forth my people the children of Israel out of Egypt" (3:10).

Moses' immediate reaction was one of incredulous disbelief. Stunned, he blurted out, "Who am I, that I should go unto Pharaoh, and that I should bring forth the children of Israel out of Egypt?" (3:11). Moses, a castaway nothing in the middle of nowhere, could not believe that almighty God wanted him to confront Pharaoh and be a leader of His people.

When we are confronted with extraordinary tasks, our first reaction is always to ask who am I to think I can do this? But at such moments we must remember that it is not our power which will fulfill the assignment, but God's. Someone once said, "All that is necessary to change our world is God's ability and our availability." This was God's message for Moses, "You have at your disposal My ability. Now, I need your availability."

William Carey was born to very humble circumstances in Northamptonshire, England, in 1761. Apprenticed at sixteen to be a common cobbler, he became a Christian at eighteen and felt called of God to be a minister. Choosing to become a Baptist minister, he continued his cobbling by night while being a pastor by day. During this time he taught himself Latin, Greek, Hebrew, Dutch, and French.

Gradually Carey became convinced that God wanted him to be a missionary. It was at the time of his official appointment in 1792 that he gave us this frequently repeated motto, "Expect great things from God, attempt great things for God." Even though at the time he was an insignificant pastor, Carey was convinced that God could do great things through him if he made himself available.

Sailing for India at age thirty-two, he remained a missionary until he died at age seventy-three. In forty-one short years, Carey sparked the modern missionary movement, translated the entire Bible into Bengali, and produced translations of the Bible in whole or part into twenty-four other dialects. And, it was his social protest that was primarily responsible for the abolition in 1829 of *suttee,* the ancient Indian custom that had meant the death of every widow at the time of her husband's funeral.

Because William Carey expected great things from God, he was able to accomplish great things for God. In the words of the Apostle Paul, Carey's life demonstrated this important truth, "I can do all things through Christ which strengtheneth me" (Phil. 4:13).

God Reassures Moses

In response to Moses' "who am I" question, God gives him this marvelous promise, "Certainly I will be with thee; and this shall be a token unto thee, that I have sent thee: When thou hast brought forth the people out of Egypt, ye shall serve God upon this mountain" (3:12). Like Gideon years later, I am sure that Moses would have liked an immediate sign from

God that he wasn't having delusions of grandeur. Undoubtedly, Moses would have enjoyed the luxury of testing God's intentions as Gideon did with his sheepskin (Judg. 6:36–40). But, in effect God told Moses, "You will be assured only when you have acted. Your assurance will come when you lead My people out of Egypt and you return to stand again on this mountain."

Many times in life we want God to give us explicit reassurance that the direction we are going or our decision is the right one. But most of the time, this comes later as we look back and see two sets of footprints on our path and know the invisible God of the Hebrews has been with us. It is then we can say with the Apostle Paul, "We walk by faith, not by sight" (2 Cor. 5:7).

Recently, my two-year-old son was standing on the edge of our porch. Positioned several feet beneath him, I told him to jump into my open arms. He hesitated for several minutes demanding that I repeatedly promise that I would catch him. Yet, my assurance didn't satisfy him. It was only when he finally let himself go and jumped with wide-eyed anxiety and uncertainty on his face that he discovered I was a man of my word. I caught him. And he giggled with an exultant glee. That's the way it is with our relationship with God. It is only when we take the leap of faith and experience the anxiety of uncertainty that we discover we are held in the arms of God. Only then can our fear become joy.

God Is a Verb

Now the Exodus writer shows us that Moses is convinced that his mission is to be God's man in the liberation of his people. But to be an effective leader he also knew his authority needed to be firmly established. So he next asked, "Behold, when I come unto the children of Israel, and shall say unto them, The God of your fathers hath sent me unto you; and they shall say to me, What is his name? what shall I say unto them?" (3:13). And from the bush came the answer, "I AM THAT I AM" (3:14), or, translated another way, "I WILL BE WHAT I WILL BE," or "I WILL DO WHAT I WILL DO."

Probably more has been written during the past

two centuries about these words than about any other portion of Exodus. The giving of God's name and the mystery that it involves has been correctly seen as a cornerstone of Hebrew theology. What did God mean by this semantic mind-twister?

Obviously, God refused to give Himself a static name by which people might mistakingly attempt to capture His eternal essense. Rather than a name, God gave Moses a series of verbs, action forms, which indicate that we can only begin to discover the true name and nature of God from the toils and experiences we confront in everyday life.

God says, "I WILL BE WHAT I WILL BE." The verbs are future tense. To Moses He was saying, in effect, "You will come to know my true name only in the *action* of serving me in future days of your life. I will 'be what I will be' as we serve together."

These words also show us that the nature of God can never be revealed by a name. Rather the true name of God becomes known to us only as *we become what we will become* in the process of following God daily. It takes a lifetime of following to discover even a little bit the meaning of the name of God. For God is not a static noun. He is an action Verb.

After giving Moses His name, God told him that he must now return to Egypt and call the leaders of Israel together and convince them that God had sent him to lead them "out of the affliction of Egypt . . . unto a land flowing with milk and honey" (3:16–17). Once his authority had been firmly established with the Hebrews in Goshen, he was then to go to Pharaoh and demand that the Hebrews be allowed to leave Egypt to go on a three-day journey into the wilderness to worship "the Lord our God" (3:18).

A three-day journey into the rugged country east of the Nile Delta would put the Hebrews beyond the ring of fortifications that guarded Egypt's eastern frontier. It would also put them beyond the jurisdiction of Pharaoh, and this simply meant that since they were being held against their will, they would be free to complete their escape. Though the plan sounded simple, God warned Moses that Pharaoh would not readily consent to his demands. It would

Overcoming Fear

take God's mighty action. "I will stretch out my hand," God said, "and smite Egypt with all my wonders . . . and after that he will let you go" (3:20). Then, looking ahead to that future time when the Hebrews were allowed to leave, God gave Moses some practical instructions about what they should take with them (3:21–22).

When Moses heard all that he was to do, his faith got weak. He needed more assurance (4:1) that the Lord was with him. And so God performed two miracles of reassurance. First, He told Moses to throw his staff down. As it hit the ground, it became a snake. When Moses picked up the snake by the tail, it became his staff again. Second, God allowed Moses' hand to become white with leprosy and then be restored to normal (4:6–7).

There can be little doubt but that these signs had a profound effect on Moses. But God wasn't through. He told Moses that if the Hebrews weren't convinced when he showed them those signs, there was one more option—he would take water from the river and pour it on the ground in front of them. That water then would be changed into blood (4:8–9).

Last Ditch Objections

Now, we might think that with all of this Moses would be convinced beyond a shadow of doubt, but he still protested, "O my Lord, I am not eloquent, neither heretofore, nor since thou hast spoken unto thy servant: but I am slow of speech, and of a slow tongue" (4:10).

But again, we marvel at God's patience with Moses—and with us. In response to Moses' lame excuses, the Lord assured him that when he appeared before Pharaoh God would be his mouth and would tell him what to say (4:11–12).

Then when Moses still protested and suggested that another messenger be sent, we read that "the anger of the Lord was kindled against Moses." But even then God wasn't through with him, for He said that Moses' brother Aaron could serve as the spokesperson (4:14–17). But Moses wasn't let off the hook—he was still to be the leader—he was still God's man to stand in opposition to the mighty Pharaoh.

Often God's leaders stand before the power brokers of this world, and to the casual observer they appear fearless. Yet within them there is a civil war going on between courage and fear. I will never forget watching a documentary film of Dr. Martin Luther King, Jr. leading a protest march in Birmingham, Alabama. As a sniper's rifle cracked, as fire hoses were aimed, and police dogs were unleashed, I saw in the eyes of this brave man what could only be called raw fear. And yet he kept on marching. Despite his fear Dr. King marched on Birmingham. And despite his fear and constant quest for reassurance, Moses marched on Egypt. It isn't that godly leaders are fearless. Rather, they are men and women who admit their fears to Him—and march on anyway.

Captain Eddie Rickenbacker, the heroic World War I ace, once said, "Courage is doing what you are afraid to do. There can be no courage unless you are scared. There can be no faith without doubt; no leadership without cowardice; no victory without struggle." Moses had met God at the burning bush. It was there God gave him his commission and reassurance. It was from there that Moses began his long trip back to Egypt.

Departure from Midian

Before leaving for Egypt, Moses asked for the blessing of his father-in-law. The wise old man graciously released him of his obligations and told him to "Go in peace" (4:18). Then, in a major act of faith, Moses decided to entrust his wife and children to the care of God and take them with him into the impending crisis and danger of Egypt. Finally, assured by God that "all the men are dead which sought thy life" (4:19), Moses placed his family on a donkey, "took the rod of God in his hand," and left Midian (4:20).

One night during their journey, one of the strangest episodes in the Old Testament occurred (4:24–26). Evidently Moses became quite ill. His wife, Zipporah, reflecting the religious understanding of those ancient times decided that God had caused this illness to punish him for not having previously circumcised their son, Gershom. Taking matters into her own hands, she circumcised the boy with a flint instrument. Following this action, Moses began to recover and God "let him go" (4:26).

Scholars agree that this is one of the most ancient passages in the Old Testament and reflects a very primitive belief that God "causes" illness to punish people. Hundreds of years later, Jesus Christ was to bring a corrective element to this age-old conception. Jesus demonstrated instead how God is a God of love and healing. He doesn't cause tragedy and illness. Rather, He works through adversity brought on by natural causes to produce healing, maturity, and a deeper understanding of life and of God.

Arrival in Egypt

As Moses neared Egypt, he was joined by his articulate brother, Aaron, whom God had sent to be the spokesman. When they arrived in Goshen, they immediately "gathered together all the elders of the children of Israel: and Aaron spake all the words which the Lord had spoken unto Moses, and did the signs in the sight of the people" (4:29–30). As a result of this meeting, "the people believed." For a while, at least, Moses held their confidence and they accepted his leadership.

As will be seen, people are often fickle. Experienced leaders know that initial approval by a community can quickly turn into discontent, criticism, and outright rebellion. A person can truly become a leader only over a long period of time as challenges and crises are confronted and weathered by the leader and those who are led. The heat of these crisis events somehow soften and merge the leader and the people together. In time, trust relationships are formed.

Though Moses was initially able to gain the confidence of his people, the task of "becoming" a leader was still before him. Leaders are not instantly made in a mold. Rather they are crafted through the years by the refining hands of God.

God Works in Unexpected Ways

As we've studied this lesson, we can clearly see that God works in unexpected ways and with seemingly unexceptional people to provide able leadership for His people. One of the most vivid examples of this truth for me was one of my Old Testament professors in seminary. As a boy, he grew up in humble surroundings and certainly did not stand out in a crowd. In fact, because of a severe speech problem with stuttering, he was at times quite timid and withdrawn.

Though he wasn't articulate, this young man was blessed with a large, strapping body that was custom-made for playing football. In high school he attracted the attention of college coaches and was recruited to play football. In the midst of college, however, he exhibited another trait—a razor-sharp intellect, and he rose to the top of his class.

As his college years moved along, this young football hero began to prayerfully reflect on his vocational choices. It soon became clear to him that God was calling him to be a minister. And yet, he knew that when he stood before a group to speak, he stuttered so badly that he couldn't be understood. Along with Moses, he said, "O my Lord, I am not eloquent . . . I am slow of speech, and of a slow tongue" (4:10). However, despite his obvious handicap, he was not able to escape the reality of his call to proclaim the gospel.

One day, with fear in his heart and certain failure confronting him, he agreed to accept an invitation to preach. Mounting the steps of the pulpit, he faced his fate with the certainty of a man clambering up a ladder to the gallows. But a strange thing happened. As he opened his mouth to read his text, his words became clear and precise. His stuttering left him. And from that day on he never stuttered when he taught or preached.

For many years this great Christian man taught the Old Testament to seminary students. He made ancient words come alive. And those who learned from him left the classroom to lead countless others to faith in Christ. Because this professor believed that God could give him the power to overcome obstacles and placed his faith on the line, this one man led many to discover the freedom that is in Christ Jesus.

My professor died late in his life, ironically while standing in a pulpit preaching in clear words the love of God. With Moses, with William Carey, with Martin Luther King, he looked over into the promised land in the final seconds of his life and marveled at what God could do with a "nobody from nowhere." His life was proof that God will always provide leadership for His people.

Father, I'm glad You work in unexpected ways and through unlikely people—that way You keep me on my toes. AMEN.

WHAT THIS SCRIPTURE MEANS TO ME
Exodus 1—4

"I need relief—now." That may sound like a television commercial, but actually it is a frequent prayer of mine. So often I throw up my hands and tell God that I've put up with such-and-such long enough. I don't want to wait another minute to see the rewards of my faithfulness.

I prayed the words last month when I was working long hours to meet urgent work deadlines. I prayed them last week when I had to say good-bye to my brother who moved overseas and won't be home for three years. I felt as if my life had been one long series of painful good-byes, and I just wanted the hurt to stop.

For generations the children of Israel must have prayed for relief. They had worked, hoped, prayed for God's release from their bondage in Egypt. Although He did not act as quickly as they would have liked, their prayers reached His ears and He responded—He remembered His promise to Abraham, and He set His plan in motion that would ultimately allow Abraham's descendants to return to their homeland.

Any request that I would make seems minor when I consider the burdens that must have been borne by a whole nation of slaves. But my God has made promises to me. In Matthew He says that if I come to Him, He'll give me rest (11:28). In Hebrews He says that He'll not forsake me (13:5). I know He listens for and hears my cry. If only I were as attentive to Him as He is to me.

Elizabeth Barrett Browning wrote some wonderful lines in her poem "Aurora Leigh":

"Earth's crammed with heaven,
And every common bush afire with God;
But only he who sees takes off his shoes;
The rest sit round it and pluck blackberries."

When I first read those words I was taken aback, because every Labor Day weekend my father and I tie buckets to our waists and trudge up the drive of a deserted hillside farm in western New York. We go there for only one reason, to harvest the blackberries that run wild across the fields.

There's nothing exciting about my berry-picking days, but then there seems to have been nothing exciting about the thousands of days Moses spent tending sheep. The day that changed the rest of Moses' life, even the rest of world history, probably started like any ordinary one. But when God saw that Moses "turned aside" from his work to investigate the bush that was burning, God spoke and revealed Himself.

I wonder if we'd have ever heard of Moses if he had been so intent on his work that he hadn't gone out of his way to take a second look at an unusual sight. I wonder how many of God's messages I've missed while picking blackberries—by concentrating so hard on the mundane routines of life that I've failed to investigate a "burning bush."

But when Moses did hear God's assignment, he protested: Lord, You must have the wrong person. You can't possibly mean me. Those same feelings of inadequacy frequently engulf me. Some years ago a new job seemed to fall into my lap. I felt God was asking me to accept the position, but I didn't think I could handle it. The prospective employer was in Manhattan—the city that seemed to chew people to pulp. And the job description included plans and goals that appeared to be as impossible to me as God's assignment seemed to Moses.

I kept telling God that He'd chosen the wrong person. He kept telling me that He knew exactly what He was doing. Despite my fears, I felt peace only when I took steps toward Manhattan.

Phillips Brooks, one of the greatest preachers of the nineteenth century, knew that God always enables those He calls. "Do not pray for tasks equal to your powers," he wrote. "Pray for powers equal to your tasks." With that lifeline around my waist, I jumped. I accepted the job and I learned that the great I AM has not changed.

LESSON 2
Exodus 5–12

God Provides Freedom for His People

Lord God, Thank You for the freedom I have in Christ Jesus—help me to walk in Your freedom today, not bound by my fears or others' interpretations of who I am. AMEN.

God created us to be a free people. But the freedom that God intended doesn't imply a release from responsibility and it doesn't mean that we are not dependent on anyone. Rather, the truest freedom possible is when we enter into a relationship of interdependence with God.

In this lesson we will see how the God of the Hebrews worked through the wonders of nature to ultimately force the Egyptian Pharaoh to "let my people go." In doing this, God wasn't releasing the Hebrews from all servitude; He was enabling them to freely follow and serve Him.

As we saw at the conclusion of the last lesson Moses and Aaron were successful in establishing their credibility with the leaders of Israel in Goshen (4:31). Now the scene shifts to the royal court of the Pharaoh where Moses and Aaron appear before the mighty ruler (5:1). The fact that they seemed to gain rather easy access to the king can possibly be ac-

Doubt and Reassurance (5:1–7:7)
The Meeting with Pharaoh

43

counted for by Moses' earlier association with the royal court.

It is important for us to remember that at this time the Egyptian Pharaoh was considered by his people to be a deity—the incarnation of the sun god Ra. He was looked upon as the perfect god who could do no wrong and make no mistakes. So when Aaron boldly "told Pharaoh, *Thus saith the Lord God of Israel,* let my people go" (5:1, italics mine), his words were considered impudent, threatening, and even blasphemous. Pharaoh's attitude is one of disdain as he makes it clear that he isn't the least bit concerned about what the Hebrew's God has said (5:2).

It seems likely Aaron might have profited by some lessons in diplomatic niceties. Throwing the demands of the detested Hebrews' God into the teeth of the Egyptian god certainly wasn't a way to win friends and influence people. But there can be no question but that Aaron and Moses got Pharaoh's attention right away as he emphatically stated he wasn't about "to let Israel go."

Moses and Aaron weren't through, though, as they said, "The God of the Hebrews hath met with us: let us go, three days journey into the desert, and sacrifice unto the Lord our God; lest he fall upon us with pestilence, or with the sword" (5:3). Then after curtly dismissing the two men and accusing the Hebrews of laziness, Pharaoh issued an order that was sure to undermine Moses' position of leadership.

Pharaoh's Reprisal

Up to this time all of the supplies for making bricks had been furnished the Hebrew slave laborers by the Egyptians, but now Pharaoh told them they would have to forage for their own straw but must still produce the same volume of work.

It may help us to visualize this scene better when we understand that building materials in the Nile Delta especially were large bricks cut from the Delta mud which were dried either by being baked in ovens or by being exposed to the hot sun for months during the summer. However, for exterior walls it was necessary to use brick blocks that were made of chopped straw mixed in with the mud. For the kind of building that Pharaoh was doing, the strong, straw-laced bricks were necessary. Now, in retaliation for Moses' and Aaron's arrogance, their fellow-countrymen had to get their own straw, scrounging far and wide for whatever they could find (5:4–12).

It is immediately obvious that Pharaoh's scheme worked. When Pharaoh refused to reconsider his demands, the Hebrews lashed out at Moses and Aaron and publicly denounced them (5:15–21). And in the face of their tirade Moses is shattered. In bitterness and frustration he says in effect to God, "How could you have done this to me and Your people?" (5:22–23).

Pharaoh's Ploy Works

So often when we set out to try to rectify a difficult situation or set of circumstances, we may experience the pain of seeing things get worse before they get better. Frequently when a distraught couple come to me for marriage counseling, I will tell them that the counseling process might at first heighten their feeling of stress and conflict before it can bring peace and harmony.

Just as a fever may need to run its course before sickness is burned away, so, too, must human conflict often reach a fevered pitch before healing and relief can be experienced. We do well to remember that water must boil before impurities are destroyed. But, of one thing we can be sure, the God of Daniel is always in the furnace with us as He was with Shadrach, Meshach, and Abednego (Dan. 3).

Certainly there are moments when the most stalwart of God's servants cry out, "O Lord, why did You ever send me?" Yet, the more experienced of God's followers know that there is usually a disturbance just before the calm. And, as we walk with the Lord, we come to better understand what the Apostle Paul really meant when he wrote, "If God be for us, who can be against us?" (Rom. 8:31). When we put our trust in God's support and timing, we can stand firm even if we do not know "why" God has sent us.

In the midst of Moses' despair over the apparent failure of his first confrontation with Pharaoh, the Lord reassures him in this part of our lesson (6:1–13) and reminds him that He is indeed the God of Abra-

God Reassures Moses

ham, Isaac, and Jacob—He is the God of the burning bush—and His promises are certain. He will deliver them from their servitude and give them the land promised to their fathers.

Moses delivered this message to the people, but even with this positive reinforcement the Hebrews refused to be convinced. Yet in spite of their doubt God tells Moses to proceed. "And the Lord spake unto Moses and unto Aaron, and gave them a charge unto the children of Israel, and unto Pharaoh king of Egypt, to bring the children of Israel out of the land of Egypt" (6:13).

Next, our Exodus writer seems to move us into a diversion as he gives us a genealogical listing of the family divisions of Israel and especially those of Moses and Aaron (6:14–27). In truth, though, we can see this as a reminder from God as to their roots. God had been with them; He would be with them. Often, it seems, that we are lost in the obscurity of events—people may forget us, but God does not. And so, I believe, we see in this geneological table further reassurance from God to Moses and to us that even as He is mindful and attentive to our past, He is with us in our present and future.

As we reflect on this part of our lesson, I am reminded of a statement someone has made that we cannot know who we are until we know who God is. The adage seems to depict clearly the quandary that Moses was in. He repeatedly shouts at God, "Who am *I,* that *I* should go unto Pharaoh, and that *I* should bring forth the children of Israel out of Egypt?" (3:11, italics mine). And in effect, God responds, "It doesn't matter who *you* are! It matters who *I* am! I am the Lord, the God of your forefathers. I am the God who made the covenant with Abraham! And even as I have watched over your ancestors, I will also watch over you. Now, Moses let's move ahead into the future."

The Same Reassurance Applies to Us

God's message to Moses at this crisis time carries a powerful word for us. While there are vast cultural and technological differences between the time of Moses and our time, the godly principle remains the same. When we are confronted with what seem to be insurmountable difficulties, it doesn't matter so much who *we* are but who *God* is! We serve the Lord, the Creator of the universe. He is the same Lord who has been faithful to His people since the beginning of time, and He is with us now and will continue to be with us in our future. We can be secure in the promise He made through Jesus Christ that His kingdom—His new society—will indeed come. And when it does, we will all be freed completely from the bondage of sin and the rule of evil. It is as we now put our trust in God that we will be able to confront "the pharaohs" of our world in preparation for our arrival in the Promised Land.

New Instructions for Moses and Aaron

After giving Moses the reassurance he so desperately needed, the Lord again spoke to him and gave him instructions for his next audience with Pharaoh (6:28–7:7). In all of this the Lord makes it very clear to Moses that He will put the words in his mouth. Moses isn't to worry about what to say because God will speak through him. Also, the Lord assures him that his God-given authority has been made known to Pharaoh (7:1).

Next, though, God warns Moses that Pharaoh's heart will be hardened (7:3–5). He will be stubborn and resist Moses' demands. When we read this, it is easy to become critical of the Egyptian Pharaoh. And yet, how often even from our vantage point more than three thousand years later, we, too, resist God's instructions as to how we should react and live.

Then before moving on to the high drama which follows, the Exodus writer stops a moment and refers to the ages of both Moses and Aaron at this stage of the story (7:7). Imagine, these two "old" men were about to take on perhaps the mightiest king in the world of that day! From an outward point of view this had to be a one-sided contest. But Moses and Aaron could be confident of the outcome because they had heard these words, "And the Egyptians shall know that I am the Lord, when I stretch forth mine hand upon Egypt, and bring out the children of Israel from among them" (7:5).

We also get some chronology on Moses' life from these few words. Moses lived in Egypt as an Egyptian in Pharaoh's court the first forty years of his life. Then he became a fugitive and spent many years in the Midian desert looking after Jethro's herds. And as we will discover in the remaining lessons, he spent the next forty years of his life leading his countrymen to the very edge of the Promised Land. It was during this time they spent a year camped at the foot of Mount Sinai where God gave Moses the Law.

In his colorful fashion, the nineteenth-century evangelist D. L. Moody described Moses this way, "Moses lived in Egypt forty years as a part of Pharaoh's court thinking he was somebody. He spent the next forty years in the desert learning that he was nobody. And then he spent forty years leading the Israelites toward the Promised Land showing what God can do with a somebody who found out he was a nobody."

The Plagues (7:8–12:36)
The Purpose of the Plagues

The ten plagues which God used against Pharaoh and the Egyptians are perhaps the most popularly known parts of the Exodus story. Because of their graphic and unusual nature, they have remained in the memories of millions of people when the rest of the story has often grown dim. But, even though the storyline is familiar, we often fail to understand the purpose of the plagues.

The first purpose for the plagues is very practical. God needed a very persuasive method to convince Pharaoh to release the Hebrews. The plagues, escalating in intensity and severity, were a pragmatic way to bring Pharaoh to a state of surrender.

The second purpose for the plagues, however, reveals their primary significance. Through them God was making a statement to the Hebrews and to the Egyptians that He is the one and only Almighty God. As He was later to declare to Moses on Mount Sinai, "Thou shalt have no other Gods before me!" In other words, the plagues demonstrated the power of Almighty God and repudiated the Egyptians' gods. A little later in our story God had Moses tell Pharaoh, "For I will at this time send all my plagues upon thine heart, and upon thy servants, and upon thy people; *that thou mayest know that there is none like me in all the earth*" (9:14, italics mine). The God of the Hebrews used the

Carvings and statuary on a temple built by Raamses II at Abu Simbel. It is generally believed that Raamses II was the pharaoh of the Exodus. This means that these carvings and statuary date from the time of Moses.

plagues to demonstrate that He alone is the Creator and Ruler of the universe.

The Nature of the Plagues

Having discussed the purpose of the plagues, it is also important to reflect on their nature. The word which is translated "plague" is derived from the Hebrew root word *oth,* which means sign. The plagues were signs of God's power. But it is highly significant that the first nine plagues were used by God through the natural order of things. Why is this important to our understanding of what happened?

The Egyptians believed in magic and the occult arts. So they were always attempting to overrule the laws of nature. But the God of the Hebrews is a God who acts, not *against* nature, but *through* the laws of nature which He created. Apart from the final plague, the death of the eldest child among Egyptian families, we have in the first nine plagues a God-inspired intensification and heightening of natural calamities that have plagued Egypt through the centuries.

Now, this fact is not an attempt to explain away miracles or the divine intervention of God. On the contrary, we see in all of this how God works through the laws of nature and the events of history to bring about His signs and wonders. It is true that even with our present scientific knowledge we cannot often explain His signs any more than the Egyptian magicians could duplicate them. But we understand that God uses the natural order of His creation to demonstrate His greatness. Our faith is based not on hocus-pocus magic. Rather, it is a faith based on a God who works within the bounds of created order and natural law which He has conceived.

God Confronts the Magician

As Moses and Aaron reluctantly prepared to face Pharaoh again, the Lord forewarned them that Pharaoh would demand a miraculous sign demonstrating the power of the Hebrew God. When that happened, the Lord told Aaron that he was to throw his rod on the ground, and when he did that the rod would become a snake (7:9).

Just as predicted Pharaoh demanded a demonstration of God's power. In response Aaron threw down his staff and it became a writing snake (7:10). But then, on Pharaoh's instructions, the Egyptian magicians threw their rods on the ground, and they, too, became snakes. For a moment it seemed the stakes were even, but then an amazing thing happened as "Aaron's rod swallowed up their rods" (7:11–12). Through this action God was making it clear that He would destroy the credibility of the gods of Egypt. In spite of this, though, Pharaoh was not impressed, and he curtly dismissed Moses and Aaron from his presence.

The First Plague

We're not given a clue as to the reaction of Moses and Aaron to Pharaoh's "hardened heart," but the action picks up quickly as God gives them instructions for the next morning. They were to go to the Nile River. There they would find Pharaoh either bathing or performing some act of religious worship. They were once again to declare that their God was supreme and Pharaoh was to let the Hebrews go. If he refused, Aaron was to strike the river waters with his rod and they would turn into blood (7:14–18).

The scenario unfolded. Pharaoh refused to listen. Moses and Aaron acted just as God had told them to, "and all the waters that were in the river were turned to blood"—the fish died and the river smelled of dead fish (7:19–21).

The Egyptians considered the Nile River to be a god. Its waters nourished the land. There was life along the banks of the Nile from its headwaters to the sea. It was the Nile that determined the health and welfare of the entire nation. This first plague was a direct attack against all that the Egyptians held dear.

How is this plague to be explained? This has been the subject of much discussion. There are those who believe that when Aaron's rod struck the water, the river became blood. And certainly God has the power to do just that. In fact, it is clear that the Hebrew word used here can only be translated "blood."

Other scholars attribute this to a marvel of nature that occurs annually as the Nile waters are invaded at flood season for a time by fungi and infusoria that give a brownish red color to the river and make the water completely unpalatable and polluted. But whatever the method God used, the effect was the same. The Hebrews' God had power over the mighty Nile.

But then on command, the Egyptian magicians were able to duplicate Moses' and Aaron's results, and Pharaoh remained stubborn and refused to give in. But for seven more days the river ran red and was unfit to drink (7:22–25).

The Second Plague

Pharaoh's stubbornness brought on the threat of the second plague (8:1–15). Unless the king relented the Nile would belch up a vast throng of frogs that would cover the land and invade the people's homes. This is exactly what happened. Once again God had struck out at the Egyptian's gods. For in those times frogs were associated with Hecat, the goddess who aided women in childbirth.

Now, when the Nile was undrinkable, Pharaoh had been able to manage, but with his palace and bedchamber invaded by the pesky frogs, that was another matter. Even though his magicians were somehow able to duplicate what was done, Pharaoh, for the first time, was anxious to negotiate with Moses. "Then Pharaoh called for Moses and Aaron, and said, Intreat the Lord, that he may take away the frogs from me, and from my people; and I will let the people go, that they may do sacrifice unto the Lord" (8:8).

In response to Pharaoh's promise, the frogs were eliminated. They "died out of the houses, out of the villages, and out of the fields. And they gathered them together upon heaps: and the land stank" (8:13–14). But now Pharaoh changed his mind and broke his promise.

The Third Plague

The stage is now set for the third plague (8:16–19). God tells Moses to have Aaron "smite the dust of the land" with his rod. And our writer says the dust "became lice in man, and in beast; all the dust of the land became lice throughout all the land of Egypt" (8:17). The Hebrew word translated "lice" in our text has also been translated mosquitos, maggots, fleas, gnats. Whatever they were, these insect pests invaded their bodies as the frogs had penetrated every part of their homes.

This time, though, the Egyptian magicians were unable to duplicate the feat, readily admitting, "This is the finger of God"—that is, something their magic and their gods could not do. Yet, we read that Pharaoh continued to be stubborn and didn't listen either to his own magicians or to Moses and Aaron (8:19).

It doesn't seem likely, though, that the Egyptian magicians had a conversion experience. It is more probable that they were really saying it was "the finger of god" or of luck or of fate or chance. It was something they just didn't understand.

We're prone to react in a similar way. When we see evidence of God's power working in our lives, we're inclined to attribute it to chance or fate. I remember so well praying one time that a book manuscript I had written would be accepted by the publisher. When the letter of acceptance came I automatically thanked God. Yet, the very next day when I shared my good news with a friend and she congratulated me, I found myself saying, "Yeah, I guess I've really been lucky. It was one of those freak occurrences where things just worked out." Down deep in my heart I knew the Lord had answered my prayer, but publicly I turned into an Egyptian magician and with false modesty I attributed the power of God to chance and happenstance.

God Protects His People in Goshen

The first three plagues attacked the Egyptians' religious establishment and showed the power of the court magicians to be limited. Yet, Pharaoh, raised from birth to believe that he himself was a god, remained obstinate and defiant.

In the next three plagues, the pressure on Pharaoh and the Egyptian people is intensified. The first three plagues were characterized by nuisance and serious inconvenience. But, the next set of three plagues involved physical suffering and the actual loss of animal life. Most significantly, the Hebrews living in the northern region of Goshen are spared and protected from the plagues. So the control and sovereignty of God is heightened as He protects His own people (8:22–23).

The Fourth Plague

In the fourth plague Pharaoh is again confronted on the bank of the Nile. He is told that due to his obstinancy a swarm of stinging and disease-bearing flies would descend upon Egypt, but the Hebrews would not be affected by the flies (8:16–32).

Stinging flies are a common pest in Egypt. Swarms of flies are often brought up by the south wind, and they frequently carry the germs of contagious diseases such as ophthalmia and diphtheria. Such swarms of flies force people to retreat inside and work must stop. Intensified by the power of God, such a swarm of flies came upon Egypt that "the land was corrupted [ruined] by reason of the swarm of flies" (8:24). The Egyptians were forced to stay locked up inside their infested houses and suffer in stifling confinement.

Under this pressure Pharaoh began to relent. He called Moses and Aaron into his presence and said, "Go ye, sacrifice to your God *in the land*" (8:25, italics mine). In other words, Pharaoh now gave his permission for the Hebrews to take time from their work to worship and offer sacrifices to God, but they must do it within Egypt's borders. Moses knew that Pharaoh was weakening. But he also knew that their ritual of worship would offend their Egyptian neighbors, so he stood firm in his insistence that they travel a three-day journey into the wilderness area east of Egypt's borders (8:26–27).

Finally, Pharaoh consented for them to leave and even asked them to pray for him. But then when Moses agreed and God removed the plague of flies, Pharaoh was stubborn again and refused to let the Hebrews go.

The Fifth Plague

Once again, Pharaoh had broken his promise. Now, God took sterner measures. Not wanting to inflict suffering unnecessarily, God sent Moses and Aaron to warn Pharaoh that if he didn't relent and let the people go, a severe and fatal epidemic would strike the Egyptian's livestock (9:1–7). But in spite of the warning Pharaoh refused to give in.

In a few words, the Exodus writer describes the

carnage, "And the Lord did that thing on the morrow, and all the cattle of Egypt died: but of the cattle of the children of Israel died not one" (9:6). The death of animal life was a blow to the religious sensitivities of the Egyptians. Their religion was animistic—they believed the spirits of the gods were present in animals, who were considered sacred. So, when animal life was affected by the plagues brought on by the Hebrews' God, there was a growing awareness that He was greater than their gods.

In spite of the devastation Pharaoh remained obstinate. He didn't even offer to negotiate with Moses and Aaron.

The Sixth Plague

Once again, Pharaoh's stubbornness caused God to act. This time Moses and Aaron appear before Pharaoh, and in response to God's instructions Moses throws handfuls of ashes up in the air. As God had predicted, the ashes became a fine dust and caused boils to break out on the people and the animals (9:8–12).

Our storyteller makes the point that the magicians and all the Egyptians were plagued with boils (9:11), and while he doesn't say so specifically, the point is made that the Hebrews in the land of Goshen were free of the sores. Neither they nor their livestock were affected. Very graphically God was demonstrating to the Egyptians His ability to control nature and to protect His people. Even though they were slaves, the power of God was at their disposal.

When we think of how God protected His people from the plagues while the nonbelieving Egyptians were brought to despair, a clear parallel for the Christian emerges. Obviously, the Christian is no more protected from tragedies and trials in life than is the non-Christian. Christians and non-Christians alike die of disease, suffer abuse, endure warfare, and are subject to every kind of hardship. In our modern world the Christian doesn't have the luxury of safety in a personal Goshen. As Jesus said, God makes "his sun to rise on the evil and on the good, and sendeth rain on the just and on the unjust" (Matt. 5:45). As Christians we're not assured of special treatment in life.

However, having said this, there is another paradoxical side to this truth. While as Christians, we're not protected from calamity, we are given a special ability to endure and overcome adversity so that we are not conquered by the "plagues" of life. In effect, Christians do have a spiritual Goshen in which we can take refuge.

The Apostle Paul was a man who was clearly not protected from the plagues of life. As he said, "Of the Jews five times received I forty stripes save one. Thrice was I beaten with rods, once was I stoned, thrice I suffered shipwreck, a night and a day I have been in the deep; In journeyings often, in perils of waters, in perils of robbers, in perils by mine own countrymen, in perils by the heathen, in perils in the city, in perils in the wilderness, in perils in the sea, in perils among false brethren; In weariness and painfulness, in watchings often, in hunger and thirst, in fastings often, in cold and nakedness" (2 Cor. 11:24–27). If anyone had experienced the calamities of life, it was Paul.

And yet this beleaguered Apostle could say at the same time, "Who shall separate us from the love of Christ? shall tribulation, or distress, or persecution, or famine, or nakedness, or peril, or sword? . . . Nay, in all these things we are more than conquerors through him that loved us. For I am persuaded, that neither death, nor life, nor angels, nor principalities, nor powers, nor things present, nor things to come, Nor height, nor depth, nor any other creature, shall be able to separate us from the love of God, which is in Christ Jesus our Lord" (Rom. 8:35, 37–39). Obviously, in the midst of persecution, Paul had learned a great spiritual truth: though we are confronted with plagues in life, the power of God's Holy Spirit assures us that we can be "more than conquerors" through Christ. In other words, there is a "spiritual Goshen" we can live in if we allow God's Spirit to control our lives.

I once knew a woman who was imprisoned in a concentration camp during World War II. She was abused by her captors and kept on a near starvation diet. After two years of such treatment she had grown close to physical collapse. One day as she hobbled down a muddy and rutted path to her squalid quarters, she saw a prison guard leering at her. Very quietly but firmly she stared him straight in the eye and said, "You may take my life away, but you can never take my faith in Jesus Christ away!" She knew that she might be enslaved by her prison guards, but she was protected from destruction because nothing could "separate her from the love of God, which is in Christ Jesus our Lord." In the midst of life's plagues, God provides a spiritual Goshen for His people.

After having endured six tormenting plagues in which his people had suffered, animals had died, and the magicians had been defeated, Pharaoh yet remained defiant. Consequently, God lifted all restraints and declared, "For now I will stretch out my hand, that I may smite thee and thy people with pestilence; and thou shalt be cut off from the earth" (9:15). This fearsome threat sets the stage for the next three plagues that would move Pharaoh to the point of complying with Moses' demands.

A Fearsome Word from God

Following the sixth plague of boils, God struck at the very heart of Egyptian economy. In the seventh plague Moses was instructed to stretch his rod toward heaven and in response a great and unprecedented hailstorm would ravage the land (9:13–35). But first, Moses was instructed to give the Egyptian people a twenty-four-hour warning of what was to happen. This would give them the opportunity to bring their families and remaining livestock under shelter (9:18–21).

The Seventh Plague

Even though hail was quite common at the time in Canaan, it was, and is, extremely rare in Egypt. Also rain is rare in Egypt. For example, in the Delta region near the Mediterranean coast the average annual rainfall is eight inches. A hundred miles or so south the rain in present-day Cairo averages about one inch a year. Some five hundred miles south of the Mediterranean coast at Aswan the rainfall is immeasurable. In this kind of climate pattern a pelting hailstorm would convince the Egyptians that it was indeed a demonstration of the power of the Hebrew God.

After the twenty-four hour warning, hail, accompanied by terrifying thunder and fire ravaged Egypt. The Exodus writer describes the scene in colorful fashion, "So there was hail, and fire mingled with the hail, very grievous, such as there was none like it in all the land of Egypt since it became a nation. And the hail smote throughout all the land of Egypt all that was in the field, both man and beast; and the hail smote every herb of the field, and brake every tree of the field" (9:24–25). All crops ready to harvest were destroyed.

In looking closely at the climate and crop chronology as given us in this part of our lesson we get a bit of a hint as to the possible time frame for these plagues. The first plague probably took place during the annual inundation of the Nile which begins in the latter part of June and peaks in September. The seventh plague of hail occurred when the flax and barley crops were ready to harvest—sometime between February and March. From this we can surmise that the time frame for the ten plagues was between eight and ten months. This simply means that Moses' negotiation with Pharaoh was lengthy.

In the meantime, the Exodus writer tells us, there was no hail in the land of Goshen (9:26), but back in the palace there was a terrified Pharaoh. In fact, he was so afraid that he freely admitted, "I have sinned this time: the Lord is righteous, and I and my people are wicked" (9:27). That sounds almost like a deathbed confession! Then he added, "Intreat the Lord (for it is enough) that there be no more mighty thunderings and hail; and *I will let you go,* and ye shall stay no longer" (9:28, italics mine).

This time Moses predicted that Pharaoh would go back on his word. But Moses went ahead anyway and asked the Lord to stop the hail. Moses called it right—just as soon as the hail stopped, stubborn Pharaoh went back on his promise and refused to let the children of Israel go (9:34–35).

The Eighth Plague

Faced with Pharaoh's haughty recalcitrance, the Lord again sent Moses and Aaron to inform the king that if he didn't relent, an eighth plague would strike Egypt. As before, Pharaoh was given a twenty-four hour period in which to change his mind. Unlike previous encounters, however, this time Pharaoh's servants and advisers came to a point of near revolt. Uniform in their opinion, they complained to Pharaoh, "How long shall this man be a snare unto us? let the men go, that they may serve the Lord their God: knowest thou not yet that Egypt is destroyed?" (10:7). Deserted by his court magicians and advisers, Pharaoh stood alone against God.

Knuckling under to his advisers, Pharaoh summoned Moses and Aaron and told them that he would allow only the men of Israel to leave the borders of Egypt to worship God. Yet, he also acidly informed Moses that he realized Moses' true intent was to escape from Egypt with men, women, children, and livestock (10:10–11). Refusing to let Moses do this, Pharaoh tried to strike a compromise and release only the men.

Sensing victory, Moses again pressed for unconditional surrender and refused Pharaoh's limited offer. Infuriated by what he viewed as impudence before a divine ruler, Pharaoh angrily had Moses and Aaron "driven out" from his presence (10:11). In the face of Pharaoh's refusal, God acted once again to strike Egypt.

After the plague of hail had destroyed the annual barley and flax crops, the wheat and rye germinating beneath the soil surface was left undamaged to grow and be harvested in April. Now, however, God moved to destroy this surviving crop, leaving Egypt open to famine. Deployed by an east wind from their breeding ground in the desert region of Sinai and Arabia, a tremendous swarm of locusts descended upon Egypt and devoured all exposed vegetation.

Swarms of locusts are not uncommon in Egypt. Indeed, as I write these words early in 1987, I have read in this morning's paper that hoards of locusts are presently consuming the crops of six African nations, threatening to wipe out already fragile food supplies. The Old Testament has many references to locusts, and the book of Joel gives a vivid description of a locust infestation. But, despite its common occurrence, the invasion of locusts was clearly seen by the Egyptians as a deliberate action by the Hebrew God. The Exodus writer states emphatically that the locusts "covered the face of the whole earth, so that the land was darkened; and they did eat every herb of the land, and all the fruit of the trees which the hail had left" (10:15).

Horrified by the certainty of famine, Pharaoh "called for Moses and Aaron in haste" and admitted again that he had sinned. After pleading for forgiveness, he agreed again to let the Hebrews go (10:16–17). With compassion, Moses asked the Lord to lift the plague. God agreed and sent a strong west wind that drove the locusts out of Egypt. However, once again Pharaoh broke his promise and refused to let the people go.

The Ninth Plague

For the next plague there was no prior warning to Pharaoh. This time God told Moses to stretch out his hand toward the heavens and a thick darkness which could be "felt" descended on Egypt for three days (10:21). This was a direct assault on the heart of Egyptian religion because of the prominence given to Ra, the sun god. You remember that Pharaoh was believed to be the incarnation of Ra.

It has been speculated that once again God used a phenomenon of nature to cause this darkness. It is not uncommon in the spring of the year for Egypt to be victimized by an intense and smothering sand storm, a Khamsin, that literally envelops the country in darkness. The Khamsin usually creates a suffocating darkness for a period of two or three days.

But whatever means God used to cause the blackness, it created havoc and proved the superiority of the Lord over Ra. Pharaoh was obviously frightened and deeply troubled for he went further than he ever had before in promising to let all of the Israelites go, but he insisted their cattle and herds must remain behind. Moses balked at this demand, pointing out they would need animals for their sacrifices (10:24–26).

Pharaoh, however, refused to go along with Moses. But even more important, he evidently became so outraged with Moses that he threatened his life. "Get thee from me, take heed to thyself, see my face no more; for in that day thou seest my face thou shalt die" (10:28). Sensing that the time of final judgment had come at last after months of unsuccessful negotiation, Moses sardonically replied, "Thou hast spoken well, I will see thy face again no more" (10:29).

In reading the story of these Egyptian plagues, most of us, I'm sure, are amazed at Pharaoh's stubbornness in the face of everything that happened. Over and over again we read variations of the "hardening" of Pharaoh's heart. We just can't understand how any intelligent person could be so blind, insensitive, brazen, and deceitful.

Yet in our reflective moments, we are forced to admit that we frequently respond as Pharaoh did. There are those parts of our lives that we want to control and rule over with an iron hand. We rationalize our stubborn attitudes when it comes to material gain, personal ambition, power, and many other private desires.

This is not to say that we don't also have those times when circumstances bring us to the end of ourselves. I know I've had those moments when I was keenly aware of being pushed to the limit, that I've come to and said, "Lord, I will release my willful desires to you. I'm tired of being king. I submit my will to you as the Lord of my life." But then, so often, when the pressure lifts, my "hardened heart" moves me to take over again.

The lesson for us is clear as we think about this part of the Exodus story. Even as Adam and Eve in the garden stubbornly and willfully disobeyed God in order to "be as gods," we, in our way, share inwardly the same desire. But we have the assurance that God's provision for our salvation through Christ gives us the power to submit our stubbornness and wills to Him. Centuries after the Exodus event the New Testament writer worded it this way, "For whatsoever is born of God overcometh the world: and this is the victory that overcometh the world,

Stubbornness Is Not Exclusive with Pharaoh

even our faith. Who is he that overcometh the world, but he that believeth that Jesus is the Son of God" (1 John 5:4–5).

The Tenth Plague Described to Moses

In Exodus Chapter 11 the Lord tells Moses what is about to happen—this next plague will convince Pharaoh to let the Hebrews go (11:1).

Next, in careful sequence, instructions are given concerning the acquisition of material goods from their Egyptian neighbors. Then Moses tells the people the word he has heard from God. "Thus saith the Lord, About midnight will I go out into the midst of Egypt: And all the firstborn in the land of Egypt shall die. . . . And there shall be a great cry throughout all the land of Egypt" (11:2–6). But the Hebrews were assured that no harm would come to them. In fact, after the next plague, the Egyptians would beg them to leave (11:7–8).

This word from the Lord to Moses was passed along to the Israelites. And then Moses and Aaron warned Pharaoh, but his stubbornness persisted, "and he would not let the children of Israel go out of his land" (11:10).

The Passover and How It Is to Be Kept

Next, the Lord gave Moses and Aaron detailed instructions about the timing and the ritual for that first Passover. And they in turn passed those careful instructions on to the people (12:1–21). A careful reading of these verses helps us understand the importance of the Passover ritual as the writer spells out the exact steps to be taken in selecting the Passover lamb, when the lamb should be killed, how it should be prepared, cooked and eaten, and what should be done with any leftovers.

The people are instructed to take some of the lamb's blood and sprinkle "it on the two side posts and on the upper door post" of their houses (12:7). It was the presence of the blood on the side and upper door posts that would insure the safety of their firstborn children, for the Lord promised, "When I see the blood, I will pass over you, and the plague shall not be upon you to destroy you" (12:13).

Then the Lord made it clear that the Passover was so important that this ritual should be followed forever in all Jewish homes (12:14)—a practice that has been faithfully observed to the present time.

Next come detailed instructions about the bread that was to be a part of the Passover meal. It was to be unleavened—without yeast (12:15–20). This, along with every other part of the meal, including how it was to be eaten, symbolized haste and readiness to go in a moment's notice.

In so many ways, our Christian rituals and symbols are vital to our understanding of the faith. Observances of Christmas, Easter, Pentecost, remind us of the cornerstone events of our faith. They also serve as invaluable reminders to our children from an early age that God is to be worshiped, and His actions and teachings are to be learned, committed to memory, and reverently commemorated.

The Tenth Plague

The Exodus writer now tells us that the Israelites throughout all of Goshen followed the instructions given them by the Lord through Moses (12:21–28). Then follows the stark description, "And it came to pass, that at midnight the Lord smote all the firstborn in the land of Egypt, from the firstborn of Pharaoh that sat on his throne unto the firstborn of the captive that was in the dungeon, and all the firstborn of cattle" (12:29).

There is much about this scene that is difficult for us to understand from our vantage point more than three thousand years later. We in faith are to be sensitive to the words of the Lord as given to the prophet Isaiah, "For my thoughts are not your thoughts, neither are your ways my ways, saith the Lord. For as the heavens are higher than the earth, so are my ways higher than your ways, and my thoughts than your thoughts" (Isa. 55:8–9).

We can, however, be sure of one thing. Somehow God acted through this tenth plague to free His people from the slavery and bondage of the Egyptian pagans. He acted in accordance to His promise—and He always does.

Free At Last

In a very few words we are given the bare bones account of what must have been a dramatic meeting. The Exodus writer says that "Pharaoh rose up in the night . . . and there was a great cry in Egypt; for there was not a house where there was not one dead. And he called for Moses and Aaron . . . and said, Rise up . . . and get you forth from among my people . . . be gone" (12:30–32). They were to take all of their possessions including anything they had borrowed from their Egyptian neighbors. We read that "the Egyptians were urgent" in their desire for the Israelites to leave. They were fearful that if the Hebrews didn't leave quickly, "We be all dead men" (12:33).

Our sacred writer gives us virtually no details on what must have been high drama—the mass movement of the children of Israel away from their homes. We are simply told that the Exodus had started (12:37–38). The first leg of their journey was roughly thirty miles, but for them it was a giant step.

After many years of bondage, the children of Israel were free (12:40–41). Our God is a God of freedom. It is His will that His people be free from all kinds of bondage.

As a teenager, I had a vivid memory of a great-uncle of mine who was quite often referred to as a "hellion." His father had been a moonshiner who was killed in an altercation with a policeman when my uncle was just a boy. Embittered by this event, he became a deeply disturbed teenager who ran away from home at the age of fifteen, lied about his age, and joined the navy.

It wasn't long until devotion to alcohol turned him into an alcoholic. When he was sober, he was likeable, but when he was drunk, he was mean and dangerous. Etched into my memory is a vivid picture of a brief visit with him in the hospital during one of his "drying out" periods. It was a fearsome experience.

Much later when my uncle was in his sixties, my Baptist minister father went to visit him. Sitting on my uncle's rickety front porch my father shared with him some of his own struggles in life and then told him how a faith in God through Jesus Christ had helped him overcome his own shortcomings.

Suddenly my uncle, who had only recently been released from the hospital another time, began to cry uncontrollably. My father continued to witness to him of the power and freedom that is ours in Christ. And after a time, my uncle prayed that Christ would come into his life and save him and give him freedom from his self-inflicted bondage.

The very next Sunday my uncle was baptized, and during the remaining five years of his life he was free from the slavery that had controlled him for so long. After a lifetime of bondage and captivity, he learned that the God who gave freedom for the children of Israel in Egypt was still a God of freedom.

There are many lessons for us in these events. But above all we can know that our God, here and now in the twentieth century, is eager to free us from any and all forms of slavery. But His liberating strength can only be unleashed in our lives when we choose to follow Him and be obedient to His Word. Ultimate freedom is only found in our service to God.

Father, I'm glad to know that Your will for my life is to be free from all and any bondage. Help me to affirm my freedom in You today. AMEN.

WHAT THIS SCRIPTURE MEANS TO ME
Exodus 5—12

When I was in high school, I learned that things are not always as they seem. My younger brother was twelve when he came down with flulike symptoms that held on and on, until the doctors told my parents of their discovery: leukemia was eating away at Philip's red blood cells.

Immediately my brother started a long series of treatments and tests that caused him more pain than the disease ever had. One side effect of the chemotherapy was severe muscle cramps. I remember getting up in the middle of the night to rub his legs in hopes that his pain would be relieved so he could get a little sleep.

From my viewpoint, his condition grew more and more grave. Like the slaving children of Israel, whose plight only worsened when Moses first asked Pharaoh to let them go, I couldn't see that God was slowly, silently working out His deliverance. For months I was like Moses who protested that God hadn't delivered His people at all. I couldn't see that in my brother's body the chemicals were winning a silent and unseen battle against the cancer.

Philip is now thirty years old and as healthy as I am. He's always a reminder to me that God's battle plan for deliverance is not the pain-free plan I would have devised. But, despite appearances to the contrary, He always works to lead His people from slavery toward freedom. He always wants us to be free from the chains that bind us—even those chains that are within our own power to break.

Later in the Scripture lesson, I was struck with the fact that Pharaoh isn't the only one who has found it hard to let go of what he felt was his. Letting go is not just a problem of tyrannical rulers but for everyone, and sometimes the very thing that binds us is what we hold onto most tightly. The word *mine* has an important place in a young child's limited vocabulary, and no matter how old we grow, the word always seems to fight to hold its rank. On the other hand, "let go" seems to be a request, even command, that God continually makes of us.

Some years ago I had a landlord who continually irritated me. He came into the apartment when I wasn't home. He too carefully watched my comings and goings. In my opinion, he was overly protective of his property. (It clearly was *his* apartment, not mine.) Then, on the day I moved out, he refused to check over the empty apartment in my presence. I, who almost never lose my temper, lost it, and then carried that anger with me long after I was comfortably settled in a new city.

Months later, over a cup of coffee, I detailed to a friend every "sin" my former landlord had ever committed. The depth of my resentment must have been obvious because when I finished my litany, my friend quietly said, "You know, you have to let go of it."

That's all she said, but I knew exactly what she meant. I had clenched my fist around a senseless grudge and was holding on for dear life. My fist only lost its tension after her words—and I'm sure they were God's words—had for days dug into my hardened heart. But finally I let go of the resentment I had so desperately wanted to claim as "mine."

Letting go is hard to do, but I hope I've learned the lesson. Look what happened to Pharaoh, who didn't.

LESSON 3
Exodus 13–18

God Provides Welfare for His People

Heavenly Lord, Thank You for supplying all my needs according to Your riches in glory. I can know, by faith, that all of my needs are being supplied by You. AMEN.

As I write these words, my four-year-old son and I have been spending several days camping out in an isolated and rustic seaside cabin. Last night while we were stretched out in front of the fireplace and listening to the winter surf crashing on a windswept beach, my little boy asked me to tell him a story.

Reflecting on the simple goodness of a roof over our heads, a warm fire, food in our stomachs, and our being together, we talked about the Twenty-third Psalm. I told him about the Good Shepherd who supplies our every need so that we "shall not want." In thinking about our time together, it is my hope that in the years to come he will remember with fondness the first time he heard about the shepherding goodness of God.

All of this reminded me that there was a time in the life of a very young and emerging Hebrew nation when they, too, learned about a God who always provides for His people. Their lesson, however, was not learned in front of a cozy fireplace in a cabin at the seashore. Instead, they learned about God's protective power facing a watery wall with Pharaoh's advancing army at their backs. In that desperate place they discovered that God was with them in the midst of a burning desert when they cried out in pain through parched lips. Though their classroom was the hard knocks of experience, they came to know that their God would be a Good Shepherd to His people and would provide amply for them.

In the first part of our lesson the Lord gives Moses specific instructions about two very important religious rituals which He wants passed along to all of the Hebrew people. The first is the consecration of all firstborn children and the second is the feast of unleavened bread. These two rituals are to be faithfully observed in the future.

A God of Guidance (13:1–22)

It is made clear in these instructions that the first sons of the Hebrew families are to be dedicated to God (13:2, 11–16). In addition, the first born of all domestic animals with the exception of the ritually unclean ass were to be consecrated to God. This would serve as a constant reminder that their firstborn were spared in the tenth Egyptian plague.

It was apparently customary in many of the early Semitic religions to sacrifice firstborn sons to their deities. In contrast, the firstborn of the Israelites were dedicated to God. They were not to be sacrificed—ancient Hebrew custom provided for them to be redeemed with a money offering of five shekels of silver (Exod. 13:13, 15; Num. 18:15–16). This idea of the redemption of the firstborn with money is even practiced by some Jews today.

The Consecration of the Firstborn

The second ritual Moses gives his people to follow faithfully is what has become known as the Feast of Unleavened Bread (13:5–10). In our last lesson we read how, in their rush to get out of Egypt, they took only unleavened bread—bread without yeast—as food. This feast would commemorate that moment when the Egyptians urged them to leave Egypt in a hurry and they began their Exodus from slavery.

The Feast of Unleavened Bread

The Hebrews Start
Toward Canaan

There were two logical routes to Canaan from the Land of Goshen. The first and closest was the military road that ran north and then east along the Mediterranean coast to Gaza, referred to by our Exodus writer as "the way of the land of the Philistines." We're told in our Scripture lesson (13:17) that the Lord did not lead them that way.

Archaeological excavations indicate that this route was heavily fortified by Egyptian military outposts, which Moses would naturally want to avoid. To have attempted to lead the Israelites through this sensitive and dangerous area would have been demoralizing if not intensely dangerous.

The second logical route would have been to head due east from Goshen into the Wilderness of Shur and then cut northeast on the caravan road that led up toward Kadesh-barnea and Beersheba. This route, too, would have been heavily fortified by Egyptian outposts.

In our last lesson we saw that the first major stopping point for the Hebrews was Succoth. Now we read (13:20) that their next major encampment was at Etham on "the edge of the wilderness" and right on the caravan route to Kadesh-barnea and Beersheba. But it was at this point that, under the Lord's guidance, Moses evidently left the established routes for a more roundabout way that would ultimately lead them to Sinai (3:12).

An Important Detail

There can be little doubt but that the Hebrews' Exodus from Egypt was hurried, but we also have every reason to believe that it was well planned and orderly. One very important detail is mentioned. Moses saw to it that Joseph's request, made many years before, was followed—they brought along his body, probably mummified, with them (13:19).

Joseph had known that Egypt would not be the permanent home of his people. When they returned to the Promised Land, he didn't want to be left behind (Gen. 50:25–26). He wasn't. In fact, his body, or as our writer puts it, his bones, were carefully cared for until some forty years later, his remains were buried in Shechem (Josh. 24:32).

God's Guiding Cloud

With careful attention to important detail, our writer now tells us, "And the Lord went before them by day in a pillar of a cloud, to lead them the way; and by night in a pillar of fire, to give them light; to go by day and night: He took not away the pillar of the cloud by day, nor the pillar of fire by night, from before the people" (13:21–22).

This simply meant that while from one day to the next the people of Israel might not know the exact route they were to take, they knew that God was leading them. Many times in my experience I've felt adrift without a clear sense of direction. At such times I've been known to say, "Lord, all I want is a cloud by day and a pillar of fire by night."

Now, I should add quickly that I've never literally seen such a cloud. But I've come to believe firmly that God is with us in all of life's circumstances and that as we place ourselves at His disposal, He leads us just as clearly as He did the Hebrews in the cloud by day and the pillar of fire by night. We may have our times in the "wilderness," but even there we can be confident of God's presence and guidance.

A God of the Impossible (14:1–31)
The March to the Sea

Upon leaving Etham the Hebrews moved out into the wilderness. From this point their route is impossible to recover with accuracy. However, a widely accepted viewpoint is that from Etham the Hebrews headed south along the shores of the Bitter Lakes to Pi-hahiroth to Baal-zephon, located on or near the shore of the upper arm of the sea that connects the Sea of Reeds—*Yam Suph*—with the Bitter Lakes.

Many of our modern English translations refer to this area as the Red Sea (13:18). However, the ancient Hebrew manuscripts refer to the body of water as *Yam Suph,* Sea of Reeds, which is located north of what we know today as the Red Sea. This confusion was likely fostered by a translation problem that predates our Christian era. And while we will likely never know for sure the precise location, we can be quite safe in assuming that the site is now a part of what we know as the Suez Canal.

As the Hebrews left Goshen and headed toward Succoth, they were leaving behind the lush green of the Nile Delta. No longer would they see sights like this as they moved into the Wilderness of Shur and then headed south into the heart of the Sinai Peninsula.

Pharaoh Changes His Mind

It is possible that since the Hebrews weren't following what would appear to be a logical route as reported by Pharaoh's intelligence, that he thought they were confused or even lost. Enough time had gone by for him to reflect on their "escape," so, filled with anger and revenge, he decided to muster his army and go after the Hebrews (14:5–8).

God let Moses in on this possibility in verse 3 when He said, "For Pharaoh will say of the children of Israel, They are entangled in the land, the wilderness hath shut them in." It seems quite clear this is exactly what Pharaoh thought. And so we're told that he ordered six hundred chariots and support troops to move out toward where the Hebrews were positioned up against the water front and close them into a trap.

In reality, though, what was happening here was a final showdown between the invincible God of Israel and the Egyptian Pharaoh—between God and the Egyptian gods. Again and again Pharaoh had stubbornly resisted God in spite of the awesome demonstrations of His power. And now, even though Pharaoh had suffered the loss of Egypt's firstborn sons because of God's judgment, he was once again about to go back on his solemn promise and wreak vengeance on the people of Israel. But God had made it clear to Moses that in the coming events the Egyptians would come to see that Israel's God was indeed the Lord of the universe (14:4).

Israel's Panic

When Israel's rear guard scouts reported that the Egyptian forces were moving up fast, the Hebrews were terrified. From the human point of view, escape seemed impossible. Ahead was the sea or lake—the Hebrew word for both is the same—and behind was the enemy that had been responsible for their misery for years.

At this crisis moment, instead of having faith in the God who had miraculously delivered them, they panicked and lashed out at Moses, accusing him of bringing them out in the wilderness to die. They insisted they would have been better off staying as slaves in Egypt. From our vantage point these thousands of years later, their unbelief and lack of faith seems incredible. Without thinking we say, "If we had seen God perform all of those miracles, we would have kept the faith!" Yet in your lifetime and mine we have seen marvels of God's mighty acts that wouldn't have been believed by our grandfathers— space flights, moon landings, lazer beams, organ transplants, instant communication by satellite. And yet our faith wavers when the going gets tough.

In the midst of this mass hysteria Moses remained calm as he lectured the people with these magnificent words, "Fear ye not, stand still, and see the salvation

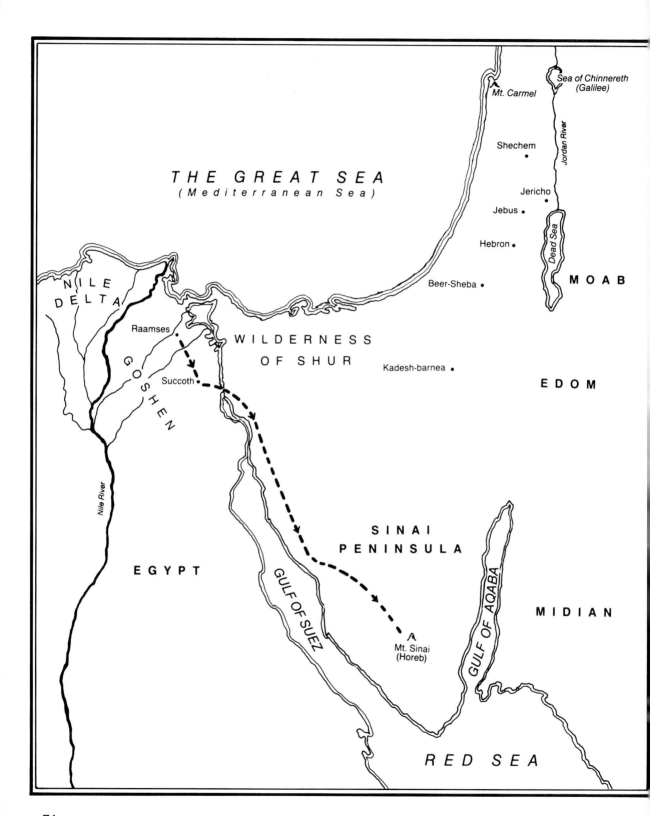

of the Lord, which he will shew to you to day: for the Egyptians whom ye have seen to day, ye shall see them again no more for ever. *The Lord will fight for you, and ye shall hold your peace"* (14:13–14, italics mine).

The Moment of Truth and Deliverance

As the Egyptian army arrived well to the rear of the Israelites, a strange thing happened. The two camps were kept separated all night by God's action. "And the angel of God, which went before the camp of Israel, removed and went behind them; and the pillar of the cloud went from before their face, and stood behind them: And it came between the camp of the Egyptians and the camp of Israel; and it was a cloud and darkness to them, but it gave light by night to these: so that the one came not near the other all night" (14:19–20).

Then we read that the Lord told Moses to stretch out his rod over the water (14:16). When he did, God sent an incredibly strong, and probably hot, east wind. This mighty wind of God pushed the waters back and dried the sea bed. Then, probably in the early morning hours, the Hebrews moved out en masse and crossed over on dry land to the opposite shore.

When the Egyptian sentries discovered that the Hebrews had escaped, the army was ordered to advance. But while they were in the midst of the crossing, the Lord acted again—causing the six hundred heavy chariots to bog down. Their axles broke and the wheels collapsed. Terror drove the well trained

OPPOSITE. While we have no way of knowing for sure the exact route the Hebrews took in their Exodus from Egypt, tradition has them leaving their homes in Goshen and traveling southeast to Succoth where they turned east and crossed the Red Sea—the Sea of Reeds. From there they turned south and slightly east along the Gulf of Suez—another name for the Red Sea—in the Sinai Peninsula. They continued to bear south and a little more east until they reached the traditional site of Mount Sinai, Jebel Musa, also known as Mount Horeb.

Egyptians to panic as they realized that the Lord was in fact fighting for the Hebrews (14:25).

In the midst of this confusion, the Lord spoke to Moses and told him to stretch out his hand above the sea bed. When he did, the waters surged back into their place, causing the Egyptian army to be completely destroyed (14:26–31).

As the Exodus writer worded it, "Thus the Lord saved Israel that day out of the hands of the Egyptians" (14:30). Once again, the Lord acted through the natural forces of His creation, but He acted, and the Israelites never forgot that miraculous deliverance (Judg. 6:8, 9, 13; 1 Kings 8:51; Psa. 78:13; 106:7–11).

During those early morning hours, the Sea of Reeds became part of a mighty act of God in behalf of His people. The night before things looked absolutely hopeless. But then, God acted!

So many times I look at the seemingly impossible problems poised to destroy our present world and I sadly shake my head. How will we ever deal with the burgeoning population explosion? Can world hunger ever be eliminated? And how about the horrible spectre of nuclear holocaust? Can we ever put a stop to such runaway lunacy knowing that we can destroy all life-forms on our planet several times over? Indeed, today's children of God face the "chariots of this world" in a no less frantic and seemingly hopeless way than did our Hebrew brothers and sisters over three thousand years ago. And so we ask, "Is there a message of deliverance in this age-old Exodus story for you and me?"

The answer, of course, is a resounding yes! We serve a God who snatches victory from the very jaws of defeat. If there is one thing the Hebrews learned it was that God is not only the Creator of this world but also the guide and sustainer of history. Just when we think our backs are against the wall, when everything seems hopeless, the winds of God will blow across the stage of history and unprecedented solutions to impossible problems will be found. We need not worry about the future of our world; it is in God's hands. All that we need to be concerned with is standing steadfast with Moses and giving God-directed guidance to our present-day problems. Instead of being immobilized by fear, we must press on and do our part.

I heard a story recently about a great fire that swept across a forest and drove all the desperate woodland creatures to the safety of a lake. In water up to their necks, a big brown bear and a great elk saw a little sparrow repeatedly dipping into the water and flying away. As they observed more closely, they saw that the little bird would gather water droplets on her wings, fly over the raging fire, and shake the meager drops onto the inferno. Very sagely, the old bear roared out to the sparrow, "You silly bird! You can't put that fire out that way!" But in response the tired little sparrow chirped back, "Maybe not! But I'll do what I can!"

I believe this sparrow's attitude should be the philosophy of all "Exodus people." Our God of History can handle the flux of the seas and the raging of the forest fires. We are simply asked to live by faith and "do what we can"! Of this we can be sure—God will provide for our welfare, even when we are faced with seemingly impossible situations.

Following the miraculous rout of the Egyptians, the Hebrews took time to worship and to praise God. Two of the ancient hymns which they sang to Him are preserved for us by the writer of Exodus. They are commonly called the "Song of Moses" or "The Song of the Sea" (15:1–19) and "The Song of Miriam" (15:20–21). More than just giving modern-day readers insight into ancient poetry, however, these hymns are a witness to the importance of worship through thanksgiving and praise. This worship should reflect the spontaneous utterance of holy awe and grateful hearts.

These songs of victory praise God for His actions in saving them from death. The ancient poets continue to inspire us. "The Lord is my strength and song, and he is become my salvation: he is my God" (15:2). The theme of these majestic songs of thanksgiving is not so much the destruction of the Egyptian

The Journey Begins (15:1–26)
Song of the Sea; the Song of Miriam

army as the deliverance of God's people from bondage and death.

I am continually impressed by the fact that before the Hebrews moved away from the eastern bank of the sea, they stopped and worshiped with praise and thanksgiving. How easy it is to become careless about thanking God for the good things that happen to us. Instead we hurry on asking for and expecting more. But here in this scene the Hebrews modeled for us the great art of worship and praise. More than a thousand years before the coming of Christ these spiritual ancestors of ours show us what it means to have an attitude of gratitude.

From the Sea to Marah

Following their service of thanksgiving and praise, the Exodus writer says, the Israelites "went out into the wilderness of Shur; and they went three days . . . and found no water" (15:22). As compared to the lush richness of the Nile Delta, the Hebrews were now plodding through treacherous terrain. The country south and east of Migdol was barren and desolate, without wells and springs. Within the short span of three days they had moved from the fear of drowning to the horror of thirst.

Then, as the situation became increasingly desperate, an oasis was finally sighted. There was water, but it was bitter and brackish—undrinkable either by themselves or their herds (15:23). And with the dispositions of spoiled children, they started to complain immediately. They had traveled from praise to complaint in just a few short days.

Stunned and hurt by the hostility of his people, a dejected Moses turned to God for an answer to his people's question, "What shall we drink?" The Lord provided an answer, proving that He is equal to the bitter circumstances of life (15:25).

The first church I served as pastor was a small country parish with a membership of seventy people. As a newly married young seminarian, I fully expected to double the membership of that church in six months and heal the wounds that had crippled it for many years. But my naïve expectations were bitterly disappointed. One night after physically separating two feuding men at a deacon's meeting, I walked outside and complained to God, "This water is bitter. I can't drink it." For the moment I was completely disillusioned.

Now, though, many years later, I look back on my two years in that church as one of the sweetest experiences of my life. It was true that the church membership didn't grow much, and the problems I found on arrival were still there when I left. But I made some lasting friendships, and learned some valuable lessons. Aided by the Spirit of God and a loving wife, I grew as a person. The bitter waters were made sweet.

Living Day By Day (15:27–16:36)

Leaving the brackish water of Marah, the Hebrews journeyed further south to Elim. Elim has been identified with the present Wadi Gharandel which is sixty-three miles southeast of the town of Suez and just east of the Red Sea. Here the Hebrews found plenty of water and vegetation. It was an ideal place to camp and must have revived the Hebrews' spirits in preparation for the journey east toward Sinai.

A Food Crisis Develops

Following their stay in comfort at Elim, the children of Israel continued to move south and east into the Wilderness of Sin (16:1). Since they had now been away from Egypt for over a month, their food supply began to dwindle. It wasn't long until the situation became acute, and the Exodus writer tells us that "the children of Israel murmured against Moses and Aaron" (16:2).

As we read the Exodus story, we find again and again that the Hebrews did a lot of murmuring and complaining even though they were developing quite a history of God's miraculous power in saving them from disaster. Again, we can't help but marvel at God's patience. Each time He met their needs in spite of their bad attitudes and lack of faith.

God Provides

In the amazing story that follows, our Exodus writer gives us a detailed account of how the Lord responded to this food crisis and established a pattern that would last all during the years the Hebrews were in the Sinai desert and until they crossed over the Jordan into the Land of Promise (16:4–36).

The Lord promised Moses, *"I will rain bread from*

heaven" (16:4, italics mine). And next Moses tells the people, ". . . *the Lord shall give you* in the evening flesh to eat" (16:8, italics mine). God makes it clear that *He will provide* bread in the morning and meat in the evening.

The Manna

Attempts have long been made to explain the manna from a natural point of view. The Exodus writer describes it as "a small round thing, as small as the hoar frost on the ground" (16:14). And then a few verses later he adds that it "was like coriander seed, white; and the taste of it was like wafers made with honey" (16:31).

Josephus, the first century Jewish historian, wrote that manna was even then available in the Sinai peninsula. And today, Arabic bedouins refer to a similar substance as *mann.* Modern scientists report that a food substance which closely resembles the biblical manna is collected and eaten by the people in this region. This particular substance is a secretion of the hardy tamarisk bush that grows in semi-arid localities in the Mediterranean region. Certain insects suck the sap of the tamarisk. The insects then secrete a substance onto the twigs of the bush that crystalizes and falls to the ground. The globules are sweet and sticky and are edible.

We know, of course, that God frequently seems to act through natural causes. But there are enough gaps in our information to leave us with a holy mystery. Of one thing we can be sure: God acted and edible and nutritious manna was the result.

The Quail

Again, many people see a linkage in the providing of quail to natural causes. It is true that during certain times of the year flocks of quail migrate from Europe to Central Africa, many of them flying over the Sinai peninsula. As a rule they fly at a low altitude and can be captured quite easily during their periods of rest.

But our writer was careful to quote Moses as saying, *"The Lord shall give you* in the evening flesh to eat."* And so our concern is not with the means God used but that He acted. Whenever He acts, we have a holy mystery.

It was the manna, though, that was the basic food

source for the Hebrews—it is mentioned many times in the Scriptures. The provision of meat is referred to only one other time, in Numbers 11:31–33.

Housekeeping Instructions for Collecting Manna

It is interesting to read just how specific the Lord was about collecting the manna. The people were to gather a specific amount for each day, according to the number of persons in the family. Only what could be consumed each day was to be picked up. The people were warned that any manna not consumed the day it was gathered would spoil—except for the day before the Sabbath. On this day they could collect enough manna for two days and it would keep overnight.

It was clear that the Israelites were to trust God for their food supply each day. There was an important lesson here for them. And this was echoed for us centuries later by Jesus in His model prayer, "Give us this day our daily bread" (Matt. 6:11). Jesus also gave us these important words, "Take therefore no thought [do not worry] for the morrow: for the morrow shall take thought for the things of itself" (Matt. 6:34). Jesus knew and taught the lesson that Moses and the Hebrews were learning in their wilderness experience—God provides for our needs one day at a time.

Day-by-Day Living

It is extremely difficult for us to live in today's world and give no thought to tomorrow. It is for me, I know. So often I find myself not really enjoying today's goodness because I'm concerned about the prospects of tomorrow. And yet as I look back over my life, I can see there hasn't been a single day when God didn't meet my needs. You notice I said "needs," not "wants."

Richard of Chichester, Chancellor of Canterbury in the thirteenth century, composed a prayer of rare wisdom and beauty that can serve as a guide for us:

Day by day, dear Lord, of Thee three things I pray:
To see Thee more clearly,
Love Thee more dearly,
Follow Thee more nearly,
Day by day.

It is in day-by-day living that deserts are crossed, mountains are scaled, God is best served, and we are most fulfilled.

Manna As a Symbol

For the Hebrews and for us the manna was far more than physical food. It is a symbol of a way of life—daily trust in God. To make certain the Hebrews didn't forget this marvelous meaning of the manna, God instructed Moses to gather up an omer (2.3 liters) and seal it in a pot that would later be preserved in a special place as a reminder forever to the Hebrew people that God is faithful to supply all daily needs. Ultimately, this pot of manna was kept in the Ark of the Covenant.

The Need for Reassurance (17:1–7)

As the Hebrews emerged from the Wilderness of Sin, they came to a campground called Rephidim (17:1). Though the location of Rephidim is disputed, the traditional site is identified with the Wadi Refayid, in the southern part of the peninsula of Sinai, near Jebel Musa, the traditional site of Mount Sinai.

Another Water Crisis

When the weary Hebrews reached Rephidim, they discovered there was no water. Driven to desperation by thirst, they began again to murmur against Moses. Some even spoke of stoning him (17:4).

In hindsight, it seems to us that the Hebrews were a foolish, fickle, and totally nontrusting people. After the miracle of the plagues, the wondrous rescue from the Sea of Reeds, being nourished by quail and manna, we would think the Hebrews would never again question God's faithfulness in meeting their needs. And yet, they doubted. And not only did they doubt, they complained belligerently.

Lest I be too critical of the Hebrews, however, I need only to view my own life to see that I, too, am one who has constantly doubted the provision of God and have demanded constant reassurance. Twelve years ago, when my wife Beth and I were married, we pooled all of our savings, and the total came to the grand sum of one hundred and twelve dollars. Three days after our wedding we moved to a new city in a distant state where I was to attend seminary. For three months neither of us could find a job. Living in a small furnished apartment, it seemed that the most plentiful thing in our kitchen cupboards was cockroaches. These were trying days—a wilderness experience.

And yet, God supplied our every need. Not once did we miss a meal or a rent payment. And now, twelve years later, we are a happy family blessed with two healthy children and are living in a comfortable life-style. Yet, despite these years of constant reassurance that God will provide for my needs, I must confess that I am at times still a doubter.

When my checking account gets low or a charge card balance grows too high, I "murmur." When sickness occurs or job dissatisfaction overcomes me, I "murmur." It seems that despite constant reassurance of God's provision, I still doubt and need to be quieted and reassured. Like an old sheep who has wandered with the shepherd for years, on dark nights I still need to feel the touch of his comforting presence.

God Provides Again

As the Hebrews complained and Moses "cried unto the Lord," God did not send lightning down to sear his whining children. Rather, he simply told Moses to take his staff, and with the elders of Israel go to a rock "in Horeb; and thou shalt smite the rock, and there shall come water out of it, that the people may drink" (17:5–6). The Lord again very graphically demonstrated to His people that He would provide for their needs. To commemorate this event for all time, Moses named the rock "Massah, and Meribah," which translated means, "Proof and Contention" (17:7).

Jesus Christ—Our Ultimate Proof

Jesus Christ came to be the ultimate "proof" that God is with us and will provide for our welfare. When a thirsty woman came to draw water from a well, Jesus—perhaps reflecting on the rock at Massah and Meribah—said to her, "Whosoever drinketh of this water shall thirst again: But whosoever drinketh of the water that I shall give him shall never thirst; but the water that I shall give him shall be in him a well of water springing up into everlasting life" (John 4:13–14). The water which Jesus gives to spiritually thirsty people is the knowledge that God is with them.

On dark nights when we wonder if we are painfully alone and lost somewhere on the periphery of our immense universe, the life and testimony of Jesus floods over us and assures us that God is with us. For this reason the early Hebrew Christians, echoing the prophet Isaiah, referred to Jesus as "Immanuel," meaning "God with us" (Isa. 7:14; Matt. 1:23).

Supporting Each Other (17:8–16)
Attacked by Amalekites

While encamped at Rephidim, the Hebrews were attacked by a group of fierce armed raiders of the tribe of Amalek (17:8), a people located in the desert between Canaan and Egypt. The Deuteronomy writer tells us that the assault was unexpected and came at a time when the Hebrews were "faint and weary" (Deut. 25:17–18). This same writer also tells us that the attack was savage and merciless and directed toward the rear of the encampment where the elderly and infirmed were camped (Deut. 25:18). In what was probably a squabble over territorial rights, the Amalekites were attempting to intimidate the Hebrews and force them to leave their territory.

The Amalekites were descendants of Amalek, the son of Eliphaz and a grandson of Esau, twin brother of Jacob (Gen. 36:12, 16). Of all the descendants of Esau, only Amalek is listed as being born of a concubine rather than a wife. This implies a low status. Consequently, Amalek and his people were considered "half-breeds" and were subordinated to a lowly role among their kinsmen.

In time, the shunned Amalekites were pushed out of their original homeland and began to lead a nomadic existence deep in the Negev and in the Sinai Peninsula. Now that the Hebrews had moved into their territory on the trip from Egypt to Canaan, the Amalekites resented their intrusion and clashed with them. Later, they frequently joined forces with the Canaanites in attempts to subdue the Hebrews. Actually, it was not until the reign of King Saul that the Amalekites were soundly defeated and were no longer a menace to Israel (1 Sam. 15).

After the initial skirmish with the Amalekites,

Moses asked a man named Joshua to form an army from among the Hebrews to stage a counter-attack (17:9). Though Joshua was soon to become famous, this is the first time his name is mentioned in the Old Testament.

Joshua was the son of Nun of the tribe of Ephraim (Exod. 33:11). As a young man, he became an assistant to Moses and ultimately assumed the role of his primary military officer. Many years later before he died, Moses, by the direction of God, was instructed to turn over the leadership of the Hebrew people to Joshua (Num. 27:18–23; Deut. 1:38, 31:14). Following Moses' death, Joshua guided the Hebrews into Canaan. Meeting fierce resistance, Joshua led the Hebrews to subdue and destroy such major cities as Jericho and Ai. And within six years after entering Canaan Joshua had conquered six tribal nations and secured the Promised Land for his people.

Joshua Leads the Counterattack

Yet at Rephidim, when Moses ordered Joshua to form an army and attack the Amalekites, there is no indication he had ever fought a battle. Moses reassured him by telling him that during the battle he would "stand on the top of the hill with the rod of God" in his hand (17:9). In other words, Joshua could be confident that God would be with him.

The next day Joshua and his men engaged the Amalekites in battle while Moses, Aaron, and a little known man named Hur, climbed to the top of a summit to watch the battle (17:10). As Moses had promised, he held up his rod, and as long as it was aloft, the Hebrews prevailed in the battle. But when Moses became weary and "let down his hand, Amalek prevailed" (17:11).

Realizing that he must continually hold the rod up if the Hebrews were to win the battle, Moses sat down upon a stone, and Aaron and Hur supported his upheld arms. In this way, Moses' rod was held high until the sun had set and the Hebrews were victorious (17:12).

How are we to understand the relationship between the uplifting of Moses' rod and the defeat of

A Practical Application of the Story

the Amalekites at Rephidim? Was Moses superstitious or did the rod have magical powers? The answer, of course, is no. Rather, from very early times it has been recognized that Moses' upraised arms and rod were symbolic of the fact that the Hebrews could win only so long as their attention, dependence, and allegiance were directed toward God. This interpretation was recognized and expressed by the early rabbis in their commentary, Mishnah Rosh Ha-Shanah 3:8: "Did Moses' hands really control the course of the battle? No! The text indicates that so long as the Israelites set their sights on High and subjected themselves to their Father in heaven, they prevailed; otherwise, they fell." In their victory that day, the Hebrews were reminded again that the ability to overcome every threatening attack was directly proportionate to their faith and dependence upon God.

There is another critical truth to be seen in this story. There was no way Moses could hold up his arms for hours at a time, in his own strength. But he was able to do it with the help and the support of Aaron and Hur. This part of the story underlines an important truth for us as we, each day, work at being effective and productive Christians. We cannot remain faithful and spiritually strong if we attempt to live out our relationship with God in isolation. The journey of faith is always made in community with our Christian brothers and sisters. We need each other, and we need the bolstering support and encouragement of others to continue on until the sun has set and the victory is won.

Even a man as stalwart and resilient as the Apostle Paul took companions with him on his missionary journeys. He needed the support and counsel of Christian friends and colleagues. It is true, of course, that in the daily give-and-take of life we all need our quiet times alone with God, but the fulfillment of our growth and mission as Christians is possible through the presence and support of others.

At a Family Reunion Moses Receives Sound Counsel (18:1–27)

As we move into this next part of our Scripture lesson, we confront one of the peculiarities of ancient Hebrew historical writing. To the Exodus writer, the flow of the story was of more concern than chronology. I simply note this in passing, because when looking at the chronology as given us in the first chapter of Deuteronomy, it would appear that Moses selected "able men," "men of truth" to be leaders (18:21–26) quite some time later after the Hebrews had arrived at Mount Sinai (Deut. 1:9–18). The whole story is a unit and in order to avoid interrupting with these events at a later time, the Exodus writer inserted them here. It is the action and not the order of events that is vital.

Even without our modern means of instant communication, news evidently traveled quite fast in the ancient world. It is likely that word about the amazing and miraculous release from Egypt and the progress of the Hebrews under Moses' leadership had been carried along the caravan route through Midian and had reached Jethro and his clan (18:1). For now, Jethro and Zipporah and Moses' two sons find their way to where the children of Israel are camped (18:2–6).

You will remember that the last time Zipporah and Moses' sons were mentioned was when they were all enroute from Midian to Egypt after Moses had been confronted by the Lord at the burning bush. Again, while the Exodus writer doesn't give us the details, it is obvious that before Moses reached Egypt, he apparently had sent his wife and sons back to his father-in-law's clan for safekeeping.

Following what must have been a joyful reunion, Moses evidently gave Jethro a detailed account of "all that the Lord had done unto Pharaoh and to the Egyptians for Israel's sake, and all the travail that had come upon them by the way, and how the Lord delivered them" (18:8). It was an impressive story and convinced Jethro to become a believer in the Hebrews' God. "Now I know," he confessed, "that the Lord is greater than all gods" (18:11). And immediately after acknowledging his faith in God, Jethro, in an act of worship, presented a sacrifice and burnt offering to the Lord. All of this was sealed as Moses, Aaron, all the elders of Israel, and Jethro sat down together "to eat bread . . . before God" (18:12).

Jethro and Moses' Family Appear on the Scene

Moses Tells Jethro the Whole Story

Jethro Gives Moses Good Advice

On the next day Jethro had an opportunity to watch Moses as he performed his administrative duties. Moses was serving as a judge and interpreter of the law for his people. All day long he listened to their grievances and disputes and acted as a mediator in their disputes. By nightfall he was exhausted and still many had not had an opportunity to talk with him.

Jethro, a man of leadership experience, was appalled by Moses' administration system. He said, "What is this thing that thou doest to the people? why sittest thou thyself alone, and all the people stand by thee from morning unto even? . . . Thou wilt surely wear away, both thou, and this people that is with thee: for this thing is too heavy for thee; thou art not able to perform it thyself alone" (18:14, 18).

Jethro was correct. By not delegating authority and responsibility to others to assist him, Moses was making three costly mistakes. First, he was being overworked and was depleting his own leadership vitality. Second, the Hebrews were being deprived of a swift and efficient judicial system. Finally, many competent people were being denied the opportunity of using their God-given skills to serve their fellow Hebrews.

Seeing the error of his ways, Moses adopted the administrative system which Jethro suggested. Choosing as assistants "able men, such as fear God, men of truth, hating covetousness" (18:21), Moses delegated to them the authority to judge problem situations that were not major in nature. Each of the new administrators was assigned groups of people to look after, "And they judged the people at all seasons: the hard cases they brought unto Moses, but every small matter they judged themselves" (18:26).

Through the help of a wise and experienced father-in-law, Moses learned what every competent and successful leader must learn—you can't do everything by yourself. For the good of everyone concerned, true ministry and service to others must be delegated and parcelled out so that many can be involved.

I remember during my college years when I was a young, eager, and energetic youth director in a church, I seemed to have an endless store of zest and vitality. In one day's time, I could lead a Bible Study, coach basketball, direct a drama practice, counsel with teenagers, and orchestrate a night-time social. But after six months of such nonstop activity, I found myself to be a twenty-year-old suffering from burn-out and exhaustion.

As I began to lose my buoyancy, and as my various programs began to lose their intensity, my pastor-supervisor recognized my problem. Like Jethro, he called me into his office one day and suggested that I form a youth council composed of adults who could help me. At first I was offended. I felt he was questioning my ability and my competency. However, I agreed to follow his advice and was quickly amazed at the results.

With the able assistance of the youth council, my program began to run much more smoothly. Important details that had once been neglected were now attended to. My own energy level began to return. But of far greater importance, the youth of the church were now being influenced by the lives of ten adult Christians and not just by one hyper Pied Piper.

God is concerned not only for the welfare of His people as a group but also for the welfare of His individual leaders. Through Jethro, God placed his blessing upon the concept of the delegation of authority. And Moses quickly learned that such a sharing of gifts and leadership was far better for everyone.

God Provides for His People

As we come to the end of this lesson, we have seen that the Lord provides for our welfare in so many diverse and wonderful ways. This doesn't mean, of course, that we always receive everything that we want. But it does mean that we will be supplied with everything which God, in His wisdom, knows that we truly need.

When the psalmist wrote, "The Lord is my shepherd, I shall not want," he was looking back over the years of his life and noting how God had always fulfilled his deepest desires. And yet, as he came to the end of the psalm, he stopped his musing on the past and began to look across the hazy vista of the future. Though he had no crystal ball to tell him of impending events, his mind spontaneously composed the words, "Surely goodness and mercy shall follow me all the days of my life: and I will dwell in the house of the Lord forever." Based on God's provision in the past, the psalm writer knew that these words of confidence were true. They can be our words of trust as well. For God always provides for the welfare of His people.

Father God, Help me to fully trust Your wisdom and love. You "only doeth wondrous things." AMEN.

WHAT THIS SCRIPTURE MEANS TO ME
Exodus 13—18

I never want to forget that thanks and praise are always the most appropriate responses to God's provisions.

There's something wonderful about corporate praise. A church my father once served as pastor was severely battered by Agnes, the hurricane that struck the Northeast in 1972. When the river dikes broke, Corning, New York, was unexpectedly overrun with water, and the church's riverfront neighborhood was especially hard hit. Seventeen people in town were killed and the river sludge peaked only after it had touched the rafters in the church's elevated sanctuary. Yet, despite the devastation, that congregation quickly gathered in another building to praise God for His protection. Their lives had been spared. Their homes and their church had been damaged but not destroyed. Help from other churches was on its way. Like Miriam, they sang of the mercies of the Lord—which sometimes come by way of our fellow travelers.

My sister Norma is a perfect example of someone who, like Aaron and Hur, provided mercy and strength for others too weak and weary to carry on. Right after the floodwaters had drained back to their rightful banks, Norma drove to the home of family friends—an elderly couple who lived near the river.

When Norma arrived ready to help them clean up, she was surprised to see the two of them standing in their front yard staring at the fresh June grass that was matted and brown with mud. When Norma greeted the gentleman, he expressed his concern for his ruined library, not for his warping furniture. While their younger neighbors had started shoveling the grime out of their homes, this older couple had no reserve of emotional or physical resources left from which they could draw.

Norma quickly saw that her strength could and would become theirs. For a week she worked at their house—heaving, salvaging, scrubbing, providing them with steady hands and bolstering their courage.

In his poem, "At the Winter Feeder,"* a friend of mine, John Leax, tells a dramatic story of the teamwork he observed at the bird feeder in his own backyard. Throughout one whole winter, three cardinals flew in to eat. At first glance, they all looked healthy, but John's field glasses revealed

---

*John Leax, "At the Winter Feeder," *The Task of Adam* (Grand Rapids: Zondervan Publishing House, 1985), p. 75.

quite a different story and explained the peculiar dynamics of the group.

One of the males couldn't feed himself because his beak had been torn off. He had obviously suffered what would have been a fatal accident if it hadn't been for his two comrades who slowly, patiently cracked open extra sunflower seeds and placed them in his open mouth. Twice a day, every day, this life-saving ritual was repeated.

I like to think that God allowed John this glimpse of natural grace just so we could be reminded of His provision. And I also believe that in this story we are reminded of our responsibility to help Him help others.

And for that reminder, I want to thank Him.

LESSON 4
Exodus 19–24

A Covenant People

Savior, Thank You for initiating and sustaining Your covenant of love with me. AMEN.

With the Hebrews setting up camp at the foot of Mount Sinai, the Book of Exodus reaches its climactic moment. Everything in our study so far is preparation for the events described in this lesson. Here we have the story of how God gave His people ten basic principles for living—the Ten Commandments.

There is an often-told story about an encounter between Mark Twain and a rather conniving but sanctimonious businessman from Boston who had amassed his fortune by unscrupulous means. While on a trip abroad, this huckster bumped into Twain and piously exclaimed that he was on his way to the Holy Land. Then he bragged pompously that he intended to climb Mount Sinai and read the Ten Commandments.

It is reported that Mark Twain chomped down on his ever-present cigar and replied, "I have a better idea. Why don't you just stay home in Boston and keep them!" Good advice!

Preparation for Receiving the Commandments (19:1–25)
"A Kingdom of Priests"

After traveling three long and hard months, the Hebrews arrived at the "mount of God" (18:5) and established the camp where they would stay for almost a year (19:1–2). The exact location of "the mount of God"—Mount Sinai—has been questioned over the centuries. But there is now popular agreement that it may well be a peak that has been traditionally referred to as Jebel Musa (the Mountain of Moses). It is part of a rugged range of mountains in the southern part of the Sinai peninsula, and reaches an altitude of 7,363 feet.

This had to be most familiar ground to Moses. He had in past years tended his father-in-law's flocks on the slopes of Horeb (Sinai), and it was on these slopes where he saw the flaming bush. It was here he encountered "I Am Who I Am"—the God of Abraham, the God of Isaac, and the God of Jacob. It was also here later that Aaron linked up with Moses, and they both traveled on together to Goshen in the Nile Delta.

Evidently, it wasn't long after the Hebrews made camp that Moses climbed the slope of Sinai and met the Lord. In this encounter Moses heard the words that would serve as the very foundation of the emerging nation of Israel, and much later, the Christian church. So important are those words that I want to include all of them here, for here is the very heart of the Old Testament.

The Lord in this scene is telling Moses what to say to the children of Israel. "Ye have seen what I did unto the Egyptians, and how I bare you on eagles' wings, and brought you unto myself. Now therefore, *if ye will obey my voice indeed, and keep my covenant, then ye shall be a peculiar treasure* unto me above all people: for all the earth is mine: And ye shall be unto me a kingdom of priests, and an holy nation. These are the words which thou shalt speak unto the children of Israel" (19:4–6, italics mine).

The first thing that God told Moses was that He wanted to be in a "covenant" relationship with the Hebrews. What is a covenant? A covenant is a solemn and sacred agreement between God and the human race or between one person and another person. A covenant is more sacred than a promise or a contract. It is a holy vow, the breach of which is regarded as a serious sin. The marriage vows are in a true sense a covenant.

To be in a covenant relationship with God was not something new for the Hebrews. Hundreds of years before, the father of the Hebrew nation, Abraham, had entered into a covenant relationship with God. Confronting Abraham in Ur of the Chaldees, the Lord had said to him, "Get thee out of thy country, and from thy kindred, and from thy father's house, unto a land that I will shew thee: and I will make of thee a great nation, and I will bless thee, and make thy name great; and thou shalt be a blessing: and I will bless them that bless thee, and curse him that curseth thee: and in thee shall all families of the earth be blessed" (Gen. 12:1–3). It was this covenant that

It was in the rugged country of the Sinai Peninsula that served as home for the Hebrews as they made their way toward Mount Sinai.

God was reconfirming with Moses on Mount Sinai. But now, God was also expanding the covenant and revealing to Moses its greater meaning.

Specifically, God was now telling the Hebrews why they would become "a great nation" and how "all families of the earth shall be blessed through them" (Gen. 12:2–3). God tells them they will become great because "ye shall be unto me a kingdom of priests, and an holy nation" (19:6).

What is meant by the term, "a kingdom of priests"? A priest is a person selected by God to serve or minister to others. Through the priest the laws of God are to be taught, the will of God proclaimed, and the nature of God exemplified through everyday living. In other words, the Hebrews were to be a priestly nation through whom all the other nations of the earth would come to see and worship God. They were to be priests serving the world.

A Heavy Responsibility

To enter into such a covenant with the Lord was to accept heavy responsibility. But now we come to an important spiritual truth. God does not call out individuals or nations for the purpose of their receiving *special privilege.* Rather, God calls His "priests" to be of *special service* to others. This meant that while the Hebrews were "blessed" above all other people to be a kingdom of priests and "a peculiar treasure" (19:5), they carried an enormous responsibility. As priests, they were to be servants and examples to the whole world.

Centuries later, when the early Christian church was realizing that they were "the New Israel" and were to be bright lights or witnesses to the rest of the world, they remembered this ancient covenant at Mount Sinai. The writer of 1 Peter told the fledgling Christian community, "But ye are a chosen generation, a royal priesthood, an holy nation, a peculiar people; that ye should shew forth the praises of him who hath called you out of darkness into his marvelous light" (1 Peter 2:9). Just as ancient Israel had received the command to be a nation of priests, so now the New Israel—the Christian church which includes all races and nationalities—would be a servant and a ministering priest to all the world.

I remember vividly my ordination as a minister at age twenty-five. It was a very special moment. With family and friends surrounding me, I felt very special, as if I had received a great honor.

However, during those moments I noticed the eyes of some of the older ministers who participated in the ordination service. I saw the twinkle of their happiness for me, but at the same time there was a look of apprehension and possibly even sorrow. They knew from long experience what was ahead for me. So, the celebration and joy of the moment and the honor of being "called forth" was colored by the awareness that the call of God is not to honor and privilege but to service and ministry.

But as the writer of 1 Peter made so clear, everyone who accepts the name of "Christian" becomes a priest. And as priests, we all are called into a covenant with God to lead a life of service, reflecting His nature to the world.

The People's Response

Following his meeting with the Lord in which he was given the covenant, Moses returned to his people and told them what God had said. When they heard that God wanted to live in special relationship with them, the people answered, "All that the Lord hath spoken we will do" (19:8). Clearly, they didn't understand fully the awesome responsibility of being "a kingdom of priests." But they liked the idea of being "a peculiar treasure unto me above all people" (19:5). So, with limited comprehension but strong desire, they entered into the covenant relationship with God.

Plans to Solemnize the Covenant

In order to solemnize this covenant, God told Moses that He would appear before the people on the third day following the initiation of the covenant (19:11). In preparation for His appearance, the Hebrews were given precise instructions. During the next three days they must maintain a state of purity, abstain from sexual relations, and launder their clothes (19:10, 15). And no person or animal was to physically touch Mount Sinai under threat of death (19:12–13).

As we read these verses, we encounter what for us

is a very strange scene. Yet, we gather from it some important factors related to the biblical understanding of God and His relationship to men and women. First and foremost the Hebrews were impressed by the holiness of God. He is not to be approached casually. His presence must inspire a sense of "fear" or sacred awe within those who worship Him.

Unfortunately, we modern Christians with our emphasis on a loving God—which He is—tend to lose the sense of God's holiness. Often our worship is casual, or even a bit flip as we forget that God is indeed the Holy One. This is magnificently expressed by the seraphim in the temple in Isaiah's vision of the Lord. "Holy, holy, holy, is the Lord of hosts: The whole earth is full of his glory" (Isa. 6:3).

New Testament Christians should not lose the sense of reverence and respect which the ancient Hebrews felt for God. We will do well when we worship to echo the words and spirit of the Psalmist who wrote, "But as for me, I will come into thy house in the multitude of thy mercy: and in thy fear will I worship toward thy holy temple" (Psa. 5:7). Their motive in worship flowed from a spirit of reverence and obedience.

Recently, I saw a group of Vietnamese teenagers interviewed by a commentator who asked them why they excelled in their school work. Without any expression of rebellion or bitterness each one said they worked hard out of respect and reverence for their parents. They didn't want to disappoint or let their parents down, and so they were the last ones to leave the study hall in the afternoon. As I watched their happy faces and examined their motives for doing the right thing, I felt their mood and attitude were symbolic in a way of what our relationship with the Lord is meant to be.

The People Meet the Lord

We come now in our Old Testament story to what must have been a most dramatic scene. With awe in his heart, the Exodus writer described the scene, "And it came to pass on the third day in the morning, that there were thunders and lightnings, and a thick cloud upon the mount, and the voice of the trumpet exceeding loud; so that all the people that was in the camp trembled [were terrified]. . . . And mount Sinai was altogether on a smoke, because the Lord descended upon it in fire; and the smoke thereof ascended as the smoke of a furnace, and the whole mount quaked greatly" (19:16, 18).

In this graphic and poetic description, the writer of Exodus clearly describes the emotional impact on those who were there. They had known nothing of thunderstorms in Egypt, and now they were panic-stricken as God's presence was felt and heard in the earthquake and in the peals of cracking thunder.

Then God called Moses up to the top of the mountain. We can well imagine how eagerly Moses scrambled up those slopes, but when he got to the top, the Lord told him to go back down and warn the people not to come too close to the divine presence on the mountain. Moses was also instructed to make absolutely certain the priests had properly consecrated themselves. It was imperative that priests and people alike be properly prepared in every way to receive the word of the Lord (19:21–24).

Perhaps the picture of a panting and hurried Moses moving back and forth up and down that mountain receiving messages and delivering them has its humorous side. But there is a lesson for us in the somewhat frantic picture. When God speaks, we must be prepared to listen.

We no longer are asked to do what the Israelites were asked to do in their preparation—wash all their clothes and refrain from sexual relations. But if we are to "draw close" and be ready to hear God, we must prepare ourselves to be spiritually sensitive through prayer, meditation, and Bible study. Then we will be ready to hear and capable of receiving the words of God.

The greatest reward that has come to me in writing these lessons on Exodus is that it has forced me into the daily discipline of Bible study. As I have been engaged in research and have prepared myself to write, I have also found that my Bible study has made me more spiritually sensitive. In pondering the ancient words of Exodus, I have heard the God of Moses speaking to me. However, without this time of spiritual preparation and Bible study, I would not have been capable of hearing the voice of God. Truly, if God is to speak to us and show us His will for our lives, we must work to be spiritually prepared to hear His voice. We must be engaged in daily prayer and Bible reading.

The Uniqueness of the Ten Commandments (20:1–2)

When Moses climbed back up to the summit of Mount Sinai for the third time and God sensed that the Hebrews were at last prepared to hear His word, the Lord presented to His people ten principles to guide them in their relationship with Him and with one another. Throughout the centuries these principles have been popularly known as the "Ten Commandments" or "The Decalogue" or "The Ten Words."

A student of ancient history is well aware that in many ways the provisions of the Ten Commandments are not unique to the Hebrews. The people of emerging Israel arrived comparatively late on the ancient world scene. By the time of the Exodus the great civilizations of the ancient Near East had all passed their zenith, but none of them could have functioned without social contracts. Many of these kingdoms had previously codified laws similar to the Ten Commandments. In fact, the prohibitions against murder, theft, adultery, false witness, and so forth were upheld by most ancient civilizations. So the question arises, "What is novel or unique about the Ten Commandments?" The question can be answered from three perspectives.

First, the Ten Commandments are never attributed to Moses personally or to any other person. The Exodus story knows nothing of a human lawgiver. The sole source of the Ten Commandments is God.

Second, in the giving of the Decalogue, God and an entire nation become parties in a covenant. This is not civil law but religious statute. And the statutes exist not only between the individual and God, but between an entire people and God. There is no known parallel in ancient history for such a national religious experience.

Finally, there are no specific penalties given for the breaking of the Ten Commandments. The motivation for observing the commandments is not fear of punishment but the desire to conform to the will of God. The impetus for keeping the commandments is not fear of retribution but a yearning to be in right relationship with God and one's neighbor.

When two young people stand before the altar of God in a wedding service and repeat the vows of marriage, they promise some very serious things— mutual support in sickness and health, constancy to each whether rich or poor, fidelity in sexual relations, and a relationship that will last "till death do us part." There will be many days in future years when within even the best of marriages a couple may be sorely tempted to break one or more of their vows. When those moments of weakness and temptation come, there may be a time when the husband or wife sits down and asks, "Why should I remain true to my vows? Is it because I signed a legal contract or made a verbal agreement before a minister and my friends?" Ultimately, the answer is no. Rather, the impetus for keeping such vows does not come from a contract or a law, but from a relationship. We stay true to our wedding vows out of a relational commitment to a person.

It was with this spirit of commitment that the Ten Commandments were given. These ancient laws are the basic statutes which Jews and Christians keep, not out of fear of punishment, but rather out of their committed love to God and to one another. The Ten Commandments are the skeletal framework of a healthy covenant relationship.

Our Relationship To God (20:3–11)

The first four commandments are directed toward the relationship between God and humans. The last six commandments are focused on the relationship of human beings to one another.

There is a good reason why the principles pertaining to our relationship to God take precedence in the order of the commandments. Quite simply, our thoughts and attitudes must be right toward God before we can begin to relate to our neighbors in the proper fashion. This simply means that we must be in compliance with the first four commandments before the observance of the final six is even a remote possibility.

"Thou Shalt Have No Other Gods Before Me"

The first commandment is the most central and primary of all (20:3). Israel's most important contribution to the religious consciousness of the human race is monotheism—the belief in one God. This was a radical departure from the religious patterns of the ancient world with their emphasis on the worship of many gods.

The Hebrews, however, recognized and worshiped one God—Yahweh—and denied the existence of any other gods.

God wants His people to understand that He alone is reliable, He alone will supply all of their needs. They are to trust only in Him. Hundreds of years after Moses, the prophet Isaiah quoted the word of God: "I am the Lord, and there is none else, there is no God beside me" (Isa. 45:5). God set clear guidelines for His people of all time. Neither the Hebrews nor twentieth-century Christians are to worship any other gods. Our allegiance is to the one true and eternal God.

It is true, of course, that we don't bow down to gods carved out of stone or wood. We don't pledge our allegiance to gods of thunder or lightning or of rivers. But we have our twentieth-century Baals—vocation, prestige, money, social position, homes, family, just to mention a few. While formally worshiping only the Lord, we allow other gods to rob us of devotion due only to the Lord.

As twentieth-century Christians, we become true worshipers when we can with all honesty acknowledge the grand truth of the *Shema* as expressed by the Deuteronomy writer, "Hear, O Israel: The Lord our God is one Lord: And thou shalt love the Lord thy God with all thine heart, and with all thy soul, and with all thy might" (Deut. 6:4–5).

"Thou Shalt Not Make Unto Thee Any Graven Image"

The second commandment continues to reveal the nature of God. Not only is He the one true God in the universe, but His attributes—qualities or characteristics—cannot be captured or displayed by any object anywhere, any time (20:4).

Since the beginning of time men and women have

attempted to make idols to represent their gods. In addition, they have set aside special objects such as trees, rocks, or mountains as places where the gods live. In the ancient Near East it wasn't generally believed that such idols or images were actually gods. Rather, it was thought that the spirit of the gods inhabited the idol or a quality of the god was depicted by the idol.

But the second commandment revealed to the ancient Hebrews, even as it does to us, that God is so wonderful no human effort to picture Him is adequate. In fact, any attempt to portray or picture God is slanderous and blasphemous.

Perhaps the best image for God used by the Old Testament writers, as well as by Jesus, is the wind. The wind cannot be seen, captured, drawn, or photographed. And while no comparison is adequate, in similar fashion, we can feel God's power at work in us and in the world. But there is no way we can capture the essence of God any more than we can box up the wind. To attempt to reduce God to something we can understand or see or feel is to make Him less than God. Then He becomes a caricature—a graven image.

"Thou Shalt Not Take the Name of the Lord Thy God in Vain"

We're told in this commandment not to use the name of God in the wrong way (20:7). The word "vain," as it is used here refers to an insincere, frivolous, or manipulative use. In the ancient world, the use of God's name in "vain" was understood in three particular ways.

First, it was believed that to utter or invoke the name of a deity produced certain magical results. In a sense this idea is related to the idolatry commandment—we can't capture or manipulate God by the use of His name.

It is true today, as it was in the ancient world, that God's name is used sometimes in taking a legal oath or in making a solemn promise. The Old Testament writers don't speak against this practice, but they emphasize the seriousness of doing it. The Leviticus writer put it this way: "And ye shall not swear by my name falsely, neither shalt thou profane the name of thy God: I am the Lord" (Lev. 19:12). In other words, a vow, a promise, made in the name of or in the presence of God was an intensely serious matter for our spiritual ancestors. It is equally serious for us as twentieth-century Christians. Our vows, our promises and commitments, cannot be entered into frivolously or with insincerity.

Then, too, God's name was often used in cursing and in violent outbursts, as it is in our time. God's name is holy, and to use it in any form of cursing is indeed "profanity" in the truest sense of the word. The thoughtless use of expletives is most certainly not the mark of the Christian.

But probably the most subtle way in which the Lord's name is taken "in vain" is when we really don't take God seriously. It is when we go through the motions of prayer and study and devotion without being actually committed to Jesus Christ. To be apathetic about our faith, to fail to be an active and positive witness for Christ, to say the words but not really mean them—this is taking the name of the Lord in vain.

"Remember the Sabbath Day, To Keep It Holy"

This is a powerful positive commandment (20:8–11). The Hebrew word translated "remember" is not necessarily a reference to memory. Instead, it carries the meaning of "observe" or "keep." In fact, the writer of Deuteronomy puts it in command form when he writes, "Keep the sabbath day . . ." (5:12).

The Hebrew word for "sabbath" actually means "to rest" or "to cease." For the Hebrews the Sabbath was and is the last day of a seven-day week, and God spelled out in careful detail for them just how this day was to be lived. "But the seventh day is the sabbath of the Lord thy God: in it thou shalt not do any work, thou, nor thy son, nor thy daughter, thy manservant, nor thy maidservant, nor thy cattle, nor thy stranger that is within thy gates" (20:10). Work was to stop on this day. The normal order of the week was to change. A day of rest and change followed six days of work.

Next, we are given the rationale for the Sabbath, "For in six days the Lord made heaven and earth, the sea, and all that in them is, and rested the seventh day: wherefore the Lord blessed the sabbath day, and hallowed it" (20:11, referring to Gen. 2:2).

For the Hebrews, more was involved in Sabbath keeping than just stopping work. Our key to understanding this idea is found in the early verses of our Bible. When God had completed all of His creation, we read, "And God saw [contemplated, reflected on] every thing that he had made, and, behold, it was very good" (Gen. 1:31). The Sabbath is a time for reflection and meditation. It is a day set aside to look around us and put our lives in perspective. It is a day for rest, recreation and worship. The Sabbath is a time to reexamine our spiritual priorities. And as we do that, for us, "God is *very* good."

For the Christian, the Sabbath—our Sunday—is meant to be a time when the routines of the other six days are set aside for rest, for worship, for reflection on God's goodness and on His Word. We are to "be still" and center our thoughts on God (Psa. 46:10).

Between the time this commandment was given to Moses and the world in which Jesus lived, many changes had taken place. With those changes came many distortions of what it meant to keep the Sabbath. Similarly, there have been many changes from the days of Jesus until now, but His words then are just as applicable to us now, "The sabbath was made for man, and not man for the sabbath: Therefore the Son of man is Lord also of the sabbath" (Mark 2:27–28).

Our Relationship to One Another (20:12–17) *"Honor Thy Father and Thy Mother"*

As we come now to this fifth commandment, the focus shifts from our conduct toward God to our relationship with each other—from the vertical to the horizontal dimensions of life. And it is natural that the first directive would focus on the relationship between children and their parents (20:12). The home has always been the beginning point of our relationships.

God is the source of all life. But the gift of life is passed from parents to children. This simply means that even as we have love for God, we are also to have love and respect for our parents.

In the ancient world, respect for parents was the norm. In Greece, the great law-giver Solon decreed that if a son didn't support his parents in their old age he would lose his privileges as a citizen. Honor and respect for parents within Jewish society has its roots in the earliest times. Even today we sense a unique bond within Jewish families that might well be the model for the rest of us.

To honor father and mother involves what we say. I find so many people in today's world who are literally starved to hear their children say, "I love you." Yes, words are important because they mirror the soul. Our parents never get beyond the longing to hear they are needed and loved.

Honoring father and mother also involves our actions—the doing of those thoughtful things that give meaning and joy to life. Giving respect and honor means being attentive and sensitive to the feelings of parents. It means listening to them. The greatest compliment we can give another person is to really listen to them. And we do this not out of a slavish obedience to a set of rules but because we love and care for them.

The only qualification ever put on this commandment came from Jesus Himself who, as a child, honored His father and mother, and during His moments of agony on the Cross had thoughts for the feelings and care of His mother.

But early in His ministry Jesus had this to say about love between parents and children, "He that loveth father or mother more than me is not worthy of me: and he that loveth son or daughter more than me is not worthy of me" (Matt. 10:37).

For me, the best explanation of Jesus' words comes from my own family experience. When my mother was in her mid-thirties, she and my father felt a strong call from God to become missionaries to the people in Southeast Asia. At the time my mother's mother was up in years and widowed. She protested strongly over my parents' decision, insisting that it was wrong and that she would be left alone and uncared for.

My mother was caught in a dilemma. But she gave positive assurance to her mother that she was loved and that she would be well cared for by her sons who were nearby. In this way my mother honored her mother as well as her commitment to God. And in time my grandmother came to accept my mother's decision and respect her for it.

This fifth commandment is most crucial, for it sets the tone for life within the family. The Apostle Paul picked up on the importance of love and mutual respect in our home life when he wrote, "Children, obey your parents in the Lord: for this is right. Honor thy father and mother; . . . And, ye fathers, provoke not your children to wrath" (Eph 6:1, 2, 4). Parents have a responsibility to earn respect and love.

"Thou Shalt Not Kill"

This sixth commandment has long been a center of controversy (20:13). It can be understood more clearly when we realize that the Hebrew word used here would be better translated "murder"—a number of later versions translate it this way.

Throughout the Bible we are reminded again and again that life is a gift of God. He breathed life into the human race, and that life is to be honored and respected. Since the days of Cain, murder has been a loathsome sin.

Jesus gave us the ultimate refinement of this commandment in His Sermon on the Mount: "Ye have heard that it was said by them of old time, Thou shalt not kill; and whosoever shall kill shall be in danger of the judgment: *But I say unto you, That whosoever is angry with his brother without cause shall be in danger of the judgment:* and . . . *whosoever shall say, Thou fool, shall be in danger of hell fire.* Therefore if thou bring thy gift to the altar, and there rememberest that thy brother hath ought against thee; Leave there thy gift before the altar, and go thy way; *first be reconciled to thy brother,* and then come and offer thy gift" (Matt. 5:21–24, italics mine). Murder begins in the heart. And it is reconciliation that heals human relationships.

"Thou Shalt Not Commit Adultery"

Adultery, sex outside the marriage relationship, has been a destroyer of spiritual and family relationships throughout all of history. "No adultery" was inscribed by God on the stone tablets, and that prohibition is as valid today as it was then (20:14).

As a pastor I am frequently in contact with men

and women who have succumbed to temptation and have committed adultery. Often, forgiveness between a husband and wife is found and a wounded relationship is healed. But I have never heard anyone who has committed adultery look back and say, "It was worth it." Instead, I've heard something like this, "The price was too high. It wasn't worth it, and I'll never do it again."

"Thou Shalt Not Steal"

To steal the property of others is universally understood to be wrong and a crime against society. This commandment (20:15) is presupposed in the giving of all the commandments. We are not to wrongfully take anything from our neighbors or from God. To do so is a sin not only against God and others but against ourselves as well.

I knew a young man in college who acquired most of his clothes through theft. For him, the game was to see how much he could steal without being caught. But it became obvious to all of us who knew him that the primary thing he was stealing was his own self-respect. Later I learned that he had also become a heroin addict. In his attempt to numb himself to his own self-loathing and guilt, he became enmeshed in self-destruction. In stealing from others, he had robbed himself of all self-worth.

But there's a subtle side to stealing that we often overlook. When we rob someone of their good name through malicious gossip, that is stealing. Stealing is failure to give our employer an honest day's work. And it can also involve holding back words of affirmation and commendation that have been earned by a loved one, a friend or an associate.

"Thou Shalt Not Bear False Witness Against Thy Neighbor"

The primary application of the ninth commandment (20:16) is found within the Hebrew court of law. It is made clear in Ruth 4 and Jeremiah 26 that every Hebrew citizen could be involved in the judicial process. Israelite law was largely administered by ordinary people who functioned as judges and appeared as witnesses. Every Hebrew citizen was to take his role in judicial matters with utmost seriousness.

The ninth commandment is literally translated

"You shall not answer against your neighbor as a lying witness." In other words, to lie, exaggerate or distort the truth as a witness in a court of law is expressly forbidden by God. In a day when capital punishment was common, such "false witness" could lead to the death of an innocent person.

At a later time, the Leviticus writer enlarged this commandment to apply to slander (19:16). To make one's judgment public—particularly if the judgment is only "half right"—is to do irreparable harm to one's neighbor.

I once heard a lady say that trying to stop gossip is like trying to unring a bell. This folksy adage is also true when it comes to bearing false witness about your neighbor. More innocent people have been cut down and harmed by the slice of a sharp tongue than have been killed or maimed by the thrust of a sword or the shot of a gun.

James, the brother of Jesus and leader of the early Jerusalem church, knew well the power of the tongue to harm people. In his letter he wrote, "Behold, we put bits in the horses' mouths, that they may obey us; and we turn about their whole body. Behold also the ships, which though they be so great, and are driven of fierce winds, yet are they turned about with a very small helm, whithersoever the governor listeth. Even so, the tongue is a little member, and boasteth great things. Behold, how great a matter a little fire kindleth. . . . For every kind of beasts, and of birds, and of serpents, and of things in the sea, is tamed, and hath been tamed of mankind: But the tongue can no man tame; it is an unruly evil, full of deadly poison" (3:3–5; 7–8).

As Christians, we are to be people who do not lie or distort the truth, whether in the courtroom or in everyday conversation. To stretch the truth, to tell only a half truth, to lie outright about what another person has said or done, violates this ninth commandment.

Each of the last five commandments is inter-connected and speaks to the fundamental rights of a free Hebrew citizen. We have seen that these rights are his life, his marriage, his property, and his reputa-

"Thou Shalt Not Covet . . ."

109

tion. Now the tenth commandment extends these rights to protection from greed (20:17).

To covet something is to desire inordinately or excessively the rights or property of others. It is primarily an attitudinal sin. However, wrong attitudes can quickly lead to wrong actions. And a greedy or covetous attitude can lead to murder, adultery, theft, and false witness.

It was with the sin of a covetous attitude in mind that Jesus said, "Ye have heard that it was said by them of old time, Thou shalt not commit adultery; But I say unto you, that whosoever looketh on a woman to lust after her hath committed adultery with her already in his heart" (Matt. 5:27–28). These are strong words. But their meaning is clear—our covetous thoughts, if unrestrained by a God-given love for our neighbor, can lead us to violate the rights of other people.

It is fitting that the Ten Commandments, The Ten Words, conclude with the injunction that we shall not covet. For in shifting the prohibitions of God from the strictly physical to the attitudinal, the stage is set for the later teachings of Jesus. Jesus saw clearly that we can keep the law to its most minute detail, but if our hearts are not right towards God and people, we have undermined the intent of the Law and the Prophets.

When Jesus was asked what was the greatest of all the commandments, He replied, "Thou shalt love the Lord thy God with all thy heart, and with all thy soul, and with all thy mind. This is the first and great commandment. And the second is like unto it, Thou shalt love thy neighbour as thyself. On these two commandments hang all the law and the prophets" (Matt. 22:37–40). To keep God's laws, not only must our actions be correct, but our attitude must be loving. We cannot love others and covet their possessions.

In that marvelous last chapter of the Book of Hebrews the writer gave us the ultimate word on "brotherly love" when he wrote that we are not to covet what others have but to "be content with such things as ye have" (Heb. 13:5). To be satisfied and

It was on the rugged peaks of Mount Sinai (Horeb) that God gave Moses the Law on the tablets of stone.

content is our right as Christians because we have the promise that God will provide for every need, and He will never abandon us. To live by His commandments is our ultimate freedom.

Our Exodus writer now paints a vivid picture of the presence of God on the sacred mountain while Moses received the Ten Commandments, "And all the people saw the thunderings, and the lightnings, and the noise of the trumpet, and the mountain smoking, and when the people saw it, they removed, and stood afar off" (20:18).

The Fear Of The Lord (20:18–21)

In this scene the entire camp of Israel is depicted as being filled with fear and awe at the presence of God. Over and over again, the biblical writers speak of a "fear" of God as a desirable attitude. But this is not a fear based on perceived harm or danger. Rather, it is a fear rooted in a profound sense of the awesomeness and holiness of God.

Here and elsewhere God's presence is announced by thunder and trumpets and lightning. The biblical writers also speak of times when, as with Elijah in the Negev, the Lord speaks with "a still small voice" (1 Kings 19:12). Other translations refer to the "still small voice" as an almost imperceptible murmur or as a wisp of a gentle breeze or as a whisper. But however God comes to us we are confronted with the awesome reality of His presence and holiness.

The wisdom writer tells us, "The fear of the Lord is the beginning of wisdom: and the knowledge of the holy is understanding" (Prov. 9:10). For the Christian, fear and trust in the Lord is essential to growth and wholeness. Yes, He is our loving Father, but He is also the holy God who created the universe and breathed life into all living things.

The Book of the Covenant (20:22–23:33)
The Need for Specific Laws

The Ten Commandments were not given by God to the Hebrews as "codes of law" as much as they were covenant agreements. This meant that they were broad, sweeping principles that should undergird the conduct of God's people.

However, in the living of everyday life, it soon became necessary to develop specific laws that would govern behavior. These laws addressed specific situations and prescribed penalties for infractions, making it possible for courts of law to make judgments based on the spirit of the Ten Commandments.

In this particular part of our Scripture lesson, traditionally called "The Book of the Covenant" (24:7), we have a description of those laws. Some of them, of course, are specifically related to the culture and practices of the ancient Near East at that time. Others have a universal application, but all are profitable for our study.

Here is a brief summary of the laws that were to govern the behavior of the Hebrews.

1. Regulations concerning the ownership and treatment of slaves (21:2–11).

2. The imposition of the death penalty (21:12–17). Four crimes were punishable by death: premeditated murder, physically attacking a parent, cursing a parent, and kidnapping.

3. The infliction of physical injury by one person to another (21:18–27).

4. The inflicting of physical injury on or by animals (21:28–36)—a person being gored by an ox, an animal harmed by human negligence, one animal harming another animal.

5. Burglary and theft (21:37–22:4).

6. Damage to another person's crop or livestock and compensation (22:5–15).

7. The liability of a man who seduces an unbetrothed virgin (22:16–17).

8. Prohibition against witches, sexual relations with animals, and idolatry (22:18–20).

9. Legal responsibility for aid to strangers, widows, orphans, and the poor (22:21–27).

10. Rules governing material offerings to God and certain dietary prohibitions (22:28–31).

11. Rules regarding right actions in situations where one would be severely tempted to do wrong (23:1–9).

12. Laws concerning religious institutions (the Sabbath and Sabbath year), feasts, and offerings (23:10–19).

13. Promises and instructions for the coming invasion of the Promised Land (23:20–33).

Over the centuries that separated the giving of The Book of the Covenant and the time of Jesus, an almost endless number of laws and regulations were added by the religious leaders of Israel. By the time of Jesus the Israelites were not so much a "people of the covenant"—concerned with right relationships— as they were a "people of the law." Their preoccupation with the letter of the law had caused them to

A Summary of the Book of the Covenant

People of the Law

113

forget the spirit of the law. Legalism had replaced authentic love for God and one another.

Jesus Came Not to Destroy but to Fulfill the Law

It was the spirit of God's Law that Jesus came to fulfill, not the myriad of legal codes that centuries of nit-picking had tacked on. And to make sure that the religious leaders of His time understood, Jesus announced early in His ministry, "Think not that I am come to destroy the law, or the prophets: I am not come to destroy, but to fulfil" (Matt. 5:17). In effect Jesus was saying here that He came to remind a judicially minded people that God isn't concerned merely with legal living but with loving coexistence. Love of God and love of neighbor aren't found in slavery to backbreaking legalism.

In "fulfilling the law," Jesus Christ demonstrated to us that God is a God of love who will go to any length to be reconciled with His people. Yes, we are to live in obedience to God, but we must never lose sight of the spirit of that obedience. Then we can affirm in our own lives the marvelous truth the Apostle Paul gave us, that anyone who is "in Christ . . . is a new creature: old things are passed away; behold, all things are become new. And all things are of God, who hath reconciled us to himself by Jesus Christ, and hath given to us the ministry of reconciliation; To wit, that God was in Christ, reconciling the world unto himself, not imputing their trespasses unto them; and hath committed unto us the word of reconciliation" (2 Cor. 5:17–19).

As Christians, we must know what is right and wrong. And yet, we dare never forget that God has "given to us the ministry of reconciliation."

Confirmation of the Covenant (24:1–18)

Following the giving of the Ten Commandments, Moses and the Hebrew leaders participated in two rites which confirmed and ratified their acceptance of God's principles for living. The first was a blood rite (24:3–8). The second was the eating of a covenant meal (24:1–2, 9–11).

When Moses told his people how God wanted them to act, they responded, "All the words which the Lord hath said will we do" (24:3). Moses then built an altar and offered a burnt offering to the Lord.

From the slaughtered and sacrificed oxen, Moses took half of the blood and threw it on the altar. This represented the presence of God. He then took the Book of the Covenant, read it aloud, and sprinkled the rest of the blood upon the people. In the showering of blood upon the altar and then upon the people, a union between God and the Hebrews was graphically portrayed. They were now of *one mind* based on the Ten Commandments and the Book of the Covenant. And they were also of "one blood," through the symbolism of the blood rite.

This blood rite is never repeated. It was a holy action once and for all times, a ritualistic bonding of God and His people.

The Blood Ritual

The second religious rite that consummated the giving of God's principles for living was the covenant meal. This ritual surfaced in the biblical story long before Moses' time—the covenants between Isaac and Abimelech (Gen. 26:30) and between Laban and Jacob (Gen. 31:54) both involved eating a meal.

A select group was present at this covenant meal—Moses and Aaron, Nadab and Abihu (Aaron's sons) and seventy of Israel's leaders (24:9). To these seventy-four people God gave a profound view of His presence (24:10). The writer says, "They saw God, and did eat and drink."

For the Christian, the covenant meal in which those seventy-four Hebrews participated is a prefiguring of the Lord's Supper. When we participate in the Lord's Supper, we are celebrating and commemorating the New Covenant between God and His people—all who are "in Christ."

The Ritual of the Covenant Meal

Immediately following the covenant meal the Lord said to Moses, "Come up to me into the mount, and be there: and I will give thee tables of stone, and a law, and commandments which I have written; that thou mayest teach them. And Moses rose up, and his minister Joshua: and Moses went up into the mount of God" (24:12–13). Moses and Joshua were told to stay on the mountain, and for the next six days a

Moses on the Mountain

cloud came down to cover the mountain, and the glory of the Lord rested on it. On the seventh day God again spoke to Moses and told him to climb up the rest of the way. Leaving Joshua behind, Moses followed instructions and climbed the rest of the way. There he stayed with God "forty days and forty nights" (24:18).

Our lesson closes with Moses on the mountain in the presence of the Lord. Here, as we will see, he receives further instructions from the Lord. In time—after more than a month—he will come down that mountain and spend the rest of his life trying to help his people live by the principles of God's commandments and laws. As he and his people discover, it is one thing to solemnly promise, "All the words which the Lord hath said we will do," and it is quite another thing to put those words into action.

Hundreds of years later another leader—a Christian—struggled to point the way to the few new believers in the Jerusalem church who were trying to forge Jesus' new society. To them and to Christians across the Roman world he wrote, "Be ye doers of the word, and not hearers only" (James 1:22).

And now, almost two thousand years, later the challenge that comes to us is that we are not just to witness—we are to *be* witnesses. Our world will know that we are Christians not just by what we say, but by what *we are!*

Abba Father, Help me to be a "doer of Your Word"—a "living epistle"—a minister of reconciliation in my world. AMEN.

WHAT THIS SCRIPTURE MEANS TO ME
Exodus 19—24

Just yesterday I was reminded of the importance of rules. Out of curiosity, I went to the first soccer game of the season—played by a first-grade team.

Two weeks ago my friend Alexis didn't know what a soccer ball looked like, and she was a typical member of her "orange" team. Last week she had attended two one-hour practices; the coach had shown the children how to kick a ball, how to score a point, and the boundary lines in which they were supposed to stay. That's all. The soccer rules would come later.

Yesterday, after the first whistle blew, the eager pack charged the ball and chased it until the end of the quarter. From the sideline, orange team parents shouted elementary commands: "Turn around. The other direction." "Goalie, kick it to *orange.*" Later in the game when the children had run themselves tired and had become distracted, parents yelled even more basic instructions, "Watch the ball."

As spectators, we adults laughed at the innocent and harmless confusion. But this morning I see the lawless soccer game in a more serious light. As I read the Law that God gave to His people, I envision the confusion and mayhem we would have if we were a lawless people.

A year ago a missionary friend who works in Australia visited Sri Lanka on his trip home to New York. Roger's time on the island was traumatic on several accounts. His last day he drove to the airport through violent riots. But even on calmer days his life was in danger. Sri Lanka has no written or unwritten traffic laws. Drivers of autos, bikes, tracks and carts simply assumed their right to the road—the whole road. Each person was a law unto himself and had only one concern: his own speedy and safe arrival at a particular destination.

The one consistent thread I notice throughout the Sinai Law is that God asks His people to be concerned with the welfare and safety of others—their neighbors and the strangers in their midst—not simply themselves. Jesus summarized the Old Testament Law in two sentences, "Thou shalt love the Lord thy God with all thy heart, and with all thy soul, and with all thy mind. . . . Thou shalt love thy neighbour as thyself" (Matt. 22:37, 39).

When my father was quite young, he accompanied his father on a short business trip. A nearby farmer was in severe financial trouble and had asked my grandfather to buy his cattle. My father clearly remembers the significant details of the day: the farmer they visited was a foreigner. My grandfather named a price and then said, "That's what your livestock are worth to me. But before we make an agreement, I want you to see if you can get a better price from someone else."

A few minutes later, as he walked away from the farmhouse, my grandfather said to his son, "I never like to do business with a man whose back is against the wall."

It's no surprise that my grandfather, who just celebrated his ninety-second birthday, is widely respected for the trait he highly values: his honesty and integrity. He taught my father a memorable lesson about God's just laws, a lesson my father has taught me. I hope I have learned it as well.

LESSON 5
Exodus 25–31

God Provides Worship for His People

Dear Father, Thank You for the privilege of worshipping You.
Amen.

Most of us, I am sure, have experienced moments when the presence of God in our lives became intensely real in a special and unusual way. Our heightened awareness of His presence may overpower us as we stare transfixed by the sight of the flaming sun disappearing into the distant sea at dusk. Or we may find ourselves deeply moved by the sweeping tones of a cathedral organ, the cry of a child at birth, or in the hushed moments of expectancy at the coming of the dawn.

Such moments are frequently referred to as "mountaintop experiences." This is where we find Moses as we move into this lesson. High up on the peak of Mount Sinai Moses has the awesome experience of being in the presence of God and of hearing His voice.

However, such peak moments come to an end eventually, as they did for Moses. The sun disappears beyond the distant sea, the organ is silent, and we come down from "our mountain" to walk once again on the level plains of day-to-day life. And so we ask ourselves, "Now that life is back to normal, how can we keep God's presence alive and vibrant?"

While it is true that we can't create artificial spiritual encounters or manipulate events, men and women through the centuries have discovered that in authentic worship the presence of God becomes real. It is for this reason, I believe, that God gave Moses explicit instructions while he was on the mountain on just how the Hebrew people were to worship Him and participate in spiritual experiences in the routines of life. For it was in their worship experiences and rituals that they would meet God and feel His presence.

The People Contribute to the Place of Worship (25:1–9)

God opens His detailed instructions to Moses about the building and furnishing of a place of worship by telling him to collect needed materials from the people—gold, silver, brass, linen cloth, skins, wood, oil, precious stones. God's temple in the wilderness, a portable tabernacle, was to be built from the offerings of the people. These were to be offerings in the truest sense of the word. The Lord told Moses to "speak unto the children of Israel, that they bring me an offering: of every man that *giveth it willingly with his heart* ye shall take my offering" (25:2, italics mine).

The Original Source of the Gifts

On the surface we may wonder how and where a group of former slaves would acquire the kind of materials and precious metals referred to in these verses. The answer is found in one of those lovely ironies that surfaces every once in a while in our Bible story. You will remember that before the last plague and before the Passover when the Hebrews were still in Egypt, Moses told the people to ask their neighbors for jewels and gold and silver and clothing. The Lord promised them they wouldn't leave Egypt empty-handed. The Lord further promised that the Egyptians would be generous with them (Exod. 3:21–22; 11:2). The people did that and came away with considerable wealth (12:35–36). So, the suppliers of the materials that went into building the Lord's place of worship were actually the pagan Egyptians.

But the authentic and willing givers were the Hebrews. Even though they had been deprived of life's luxuries for so long, they now gave willingly so as to provide a "sanctuary" where the Lord would "dwell among them" (25:8–9). In verse 9 the writer refers to the sanctuary as "the tabernacle." This is the term most of our translations use, although an occasional one uses the word "tent." The Hebrew word translated "tabernacle" actually means "dwelling place." Their portable Tabernacle was to be the dwelling place of God. The God of the Hebrews, the Christian God, is always *with* His people. He is not a distant, far-off God—He is with us in the hurly-burly complexities of our everyday routines.

The Willing Givers to the Lord's Tabernacle

Next come the detailed instructions for the building of three important pieces of furniture that were to be placed inside the finished Tabernacle. Each of these items was important for the worship ceremonies of the Hebrews.

The Contents of the Tabernacle (25:10–40)

With careful attention to detail the Exodus writer begins his description of the first item of furniture that was to go in the Tabernacle, "And they shall make an ark of shittim [acacia] wood: two cubits and a half [forty-five inches] shall be the length thereof, and a cubit and a half [twenty-seven inches] the breadth thereof, and a cubit and a half [twenty-seven inches] the height thereof" (25:10).

The Ark of the Covenant

The Ark—a chest or box—was to have an overlay of gold leaf and "a crown of gold round about" (25:11). Gold rings were to be fitted into the corners on each side into which poles of acacia wood overlaid with gold could be fitted for the purpose of carrying the Ark when it was moved (25:11–15).

The Ark was to have a covering or lid made of pure gold. This has traditionally been referred to as the "mercy seat" (25:17), however, a more correct translation of the Hebrew would be "atonement cover." At either end of the cover were gold cherubim facing each other—their outstretched wings raised to arch over the Ark (25:17–21).

NORTH

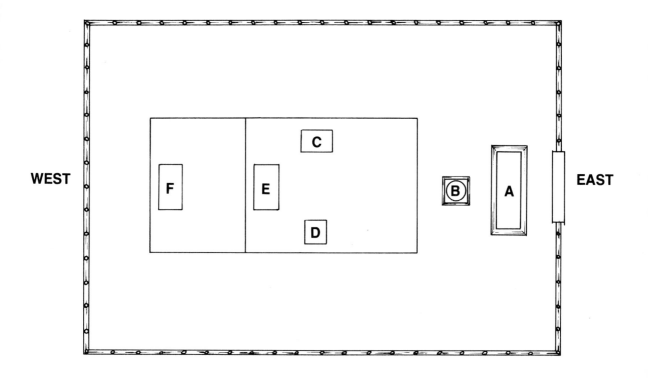

WEST

EAST

SOUTH

The drawing above gives us an artist's impression of the layout of the Tabernacle. When the priests entered through the east gate, before them was A, the Brazen Altar on which sacrifices were offered, and B, the Laver at which they cleansed themselves before entering the Tabernacle. The furnishings in the Holy Place were the Table of Shewbread, C, the Golden Lampstand, D, and The Golden Altar of Incense, E. Behind the Golden Altar of Incense was the veil that divided the Holy Place from the Holy of Holies. It was to this inner room that the high priest came once a year. Located here was the Ark of the Covenant, F. When in camp, the tents of the Israelites were positioned in prescribed location on all four sides of the Tabernacle. The place of worship stood in the middle of the camp.

The stone tablets containing the Law were to rest inside the Ark (25:16, 21). In the Deuteronomy account Moses, after receiving the Law from God on the mountain said, "And I turned myself and came down from the mount, and put the tables in the ark which I had made; and there they be, as the Lord commanded me" (Deut. 10:5).

The Ark, positioned in the Holy of Holies in the Tabernacle, was the place where God would meet with His people. Recording the words of the Lord, the Exodus writer says, "And there I will meet with thee, and I will commune with thee from above the mercy seat, from between the two cherubims which are upon the ark of the testimony, of all things which I will give thee in commandment unto the children of Israel" (25:22).

The Ark of the Covenant traveled with the Hebrews from Mount Sinai to the Promised Land. And when they finally crossed the Jordan River into Canaan it was installed in a sanctuary in Shiloh. Later King David took the Ark in a ritual procession to Jerusalem where he put it in his tent sanctuary. Finally it was installed in the inner sanctuary of Solomon's temple (1 Kings 8:1–9). From this point on the fate of the Ark is unknown. It is likely it was destroyed when the Babylonians-Chaldeans sacked Jerusalem and burned Solomon's temple to the ground. But there is no doubt but that the Ark had disappeared by the time of the rebuilding of the temple by Zerubbabel around 520–16 B.C.

The Table of Shewbread

The second piece of furniture for the Tabernacle that is mentioned here is the Table of Shewbread (25:23–30). Again the Lord's instructions are very specific. The table is to be made of acacia wood. It is to be exactly thirty-six inches long, eighteen inches wide and twenty-seven inches tall. It was to have an overlay of pure gold with a gold crown around it and would be equipped with rings and staves like the Ark, for easy carrying.

Instructions are also given for the utensils to be used on the Table. "And thou shalt set upon the table shewbread before me alway" (25:30). The writer of

Leviticus (24:5–9) tells us that on every Sabbath the priests placed twelve baked cakes of bread, in two rows of six each, and some frankincense on the Table.

The shewbread—literally, the "bread of the presence"—likely symbolized the presence of God. As Christians we are reminded of Jesus' words, "I am the bread of life: he that cometh to me shall never hunger" (John 6:35).

The Lampstand

The third item of furniture mentioned here is the Lampstand (25:31–40). It, too, was to be made of pure gold, and have three branches on either side of a center stem—making seven lamps in all. The lamps were to give light, and the instructions were that they were to burn day and night.

According to the description of the Lampstand given here, it quite likely had the appearance of the seven-branched Menorah that continues to be in use today and conveys powerful symbolism to Jew and Christian alike.

Symbolism in the sanctuary—the church—should be seen and understood by everyone who participates in worship. All too often we fail to reflect in worship on the rich heritage of symbolic objects and actions that have been passed on to us from the earliest days of the church—the altar, the pulpit, the cross, the stained glass windows, the Lord's Supper, baptism. When rightly understood each of these add meaning and spiritual understanding to our worship and praise.

Stained glass windows meant much more to me when I learned that they were intended in the Middle Ages to be teaching and learning tools. In those days the majority of people could not read, but as they sat in the churches and cathedrals, they would participate in the Bible story as it was depicted in the windows. Knowing this gave the church windows a whole new meaning for me. Now they are no longer merely objects of beauty. Instead, I see in them the drama of the Bible as God's grace comes alive in stained glass.

Since the Hebrews were people on the move—a nomadic people—at this stage of their national life, it was important that their place of worship be portable. Such being the case God's instructions for building provided for their being able to set it up when they made camp and to dismantle it when they were ready to move on.

The skeletal structure of the Tabernacle was to consist of a rectangle framework of interlocking, trellis-like boards (26:15–30). The boards in this framework were fifteen feet high and twenty-seven inches wide. They were acacia wood and overlaid in gold. The overall structure was approximately forty-five feet long, fifteen feet wide, and fifteen feet high.

This framework was covered across the top, back, and sides with ten curtains of very fine-woven linen and fastened by gold clasps (26:1–6). These curtains are described as blue, purple, and scarlet and were embroidered with cherubim (26:1). The front of the Tabernacle was covered by an elaborate gold overlaid and embroidered screen (26:36–37).

As protection for the framework structure and the curtain coverings, as well as the interior appointments, an outer covering made of ram and goat skins (26:7–14) was placed like a tent over the Tabernacle.

The interior structure of the Tabernacle was divided into two unequal rooms. The first two-thirds was known as The Holy Place. The Table of Shewbread and the Golden Lampstand were positioned here—one on each side of the room. The second room, the Holy of Holies, was set off from the first room by a veil. It was in this inner sanctuary that the Ark of the Covenant was placed (26:33).

Surrounding the Tabernacle was a large courtyard one hundred fifty feet long and seventy-five feet wide (27:9–19). The enclosure for the courtyard was a portable wall or fence composed of hangings of finely woven linen stretched over sixty posts or "pil-

The Tabernacle
(26:1–27:21)
The Basic Structure

The Covering for the Structure

The Interior Structure

The Outside Court of the Tabernacle

lars" with bronze bases. The curtained fence stood twenty-two and one-half feet high. This meant that while the upper part of the Tabernacle could be seen from the outside, everything that went on within the courtyard was hidden from view. The only entrance to the courtyard was a gate on the east end. It was a colorful linen screen that hung on four pillars (27:16).

The Altar of Burnt Offering

Inside the courtyard and between the entrance gate and the Tabernacle structure stood the Altar of Burnt Offering—the Altar of the Holocaust (27:1–8). Made of acacia wood and plated with bronze the Altar was seven and one-half feet square and four and one-half feet high. There were four horns on the Altar, one on each of the four corners. At that time, horns were symbolic of power and likely symbolized the power of God in behalf of the one who brought the offering.

The priests offered a animal sacrifice on the Altar in the morning and evening (Exod. 29:38–42). Blood from the animal was sprinkled on each of the horns and the flesh was burned on the Altar itself.

As with other Tabernacle furnishings, provisions were made for rings and poles so the Altar could be readily carried when camp was moved.

Oil for the Lampstand

The Lord's final instructions in this part of our Scripture lesson were for the people to supply olive oil for use in the Lampstand in the Holy Place. Then they were told that after the bowls of oil in the Lampstand were lit, Aaron and his sons were never to let the light go out.

The Tabernacle—Its Meaning for the Hebrews and for Us

With the building of the Tabernacle the Hebrews were assured that their God was always with them. When they moved, He was there. When they camped, He was there. Unlike the pagan gods in Mesopotamia, Egypt, and Canaan, who were "up there" and aloof, the God of Israel was with them. This same God had made His wishes known to the Patriarch Abraham in Ur and in Haran. He had been with the sons of Abraham, Isaac, and Jacob in Egypt. Now He was with them as the God of the mountain and the Sinai desert. The earth was His habitation.

Earthly tabernacles, temples, and churches are places where we worship. Yet the Creator-God of the universe cannot be contained within walls. He is with us in the busyness of our cities and in peaceful rural settings. He is a God on the move who is ever-present with us.

The ancient psalmist expressed it well when he wrote, "Whither shall I go from thy spirit? or whither shall I flee from thy presence? If I ascend up into heaven, thou art there: if I make my bed in hell, behold, thou art there. If I take the wings of the morning, and dwell in the uttermost parts of the sea; Even there shall thy hand lead me, and thy right hand shall hold me" (Psa. 139:7–10).

As representatives of God, the priests formed the bridge between the Lord and His people. This part of our Scripture lesson is devoted to a description of their clothing. It is significant to note the care God took to describe exactly how He wanted the priests—Aaron and his sons—to dress. As God's representatives in the camp of Israel, their clothing was rich in symbolism. Most of this part of our Scripture lesson is devoted to the clothing or vestments of the high priest (28:2–39)—Aaron. Only in verses 40–43 do we have a description of the clothing worn by the priests—Aaron's sons.

The Priest's Clothing (28:1–43)

The first item of clothing mentioned by the Exodus writer is the Ephod (28:5–14). This was quite an ornate vestment made of fine linen and with gold, blue, purple, and red yarn. Its shape was apparently that of a kiltlike skirt and was held in place by two shoulder pieces. An onyx stone was affixed to each of the shoulder pieces. The names of the twelve tribes of Israel were engraved on them—six on each stone.

The Ephod

Probably the most significant piece of clothing was the Breastplate of Judgment (28:15–30). This was made of the same linen material as the Ephod and was connected to the shoulder pieces and the Ephod by gold rings. It apparently was a pouch about nine inches square and was blue, purple, and scarlet and embroidered with gold thread.

The Breastplate of Judgment

The front Breastplate contained twelve precious stones in gold settings, arranged in four rows—three stones to a row. Engraved on each stone was the name of one of the twelve tribes of Israel.

The Urim and Thummim

The Urim and Thummim were kept in the pouch of the Breastplate (28:30). Little is known about these articles, and they apparently disappeared from the priestly scene quite early. They were probably a means of determining God's will. There are various conjectures as to just what this was, but references to them in the Old Testament associate them with seeking the Lord's guidance for the people.

The Robe of the Ephod

The Robe of the Ephod was evidently a long, tunic-like undergarment (28:31–35), made of blue (violet) cloth. It was decorated around the bottom with brilliantly colored pomegranates made of cloth and small golden bells which rang as the high priest moved about in his duties.

Outer Coat and Mitre

The high priest's outer coat was made of fine linen and secured with a sash (28:39). He was to wear a white linen turban or mitre on his head. A gold plate was affixed to the turban or mitre on which were inscribed the words, "Holiness to the Lord" (28:36–38).

The Priests' Clothing

In verses 40–43 brief mention is made of the clothing to be worn by the other priests—Aaron's sons. The reference is made to "linen breeches," coats, girdles (tunics), and turbans. And while mention is not made of them here, they most likely wore ephods.

The care given here and elsewhere to the description of the clothing and vestments worn by Israel's priests certainly indicates that God intended His representatives to be recognized as they went about their sacred tasks. Special attire for God's specially called priests and ministers was never meant to call attention to them but rather to signify that they are separated to lead in worship and perform other specialized duties. Whether that attire is a certain colored business suit or dress or any form of clerical dress or vestment, the symbolic purpose is to remind us that in worship and service we are to give "Holiness to the Lord" (28:36).

The Consecration of the Priests (29:1–46)

Immediately following the giving of the detailed instructions for the building of the Tabernacle and for the design of the priests' clothing, God directed Moses to consecrate Aaron and his sons to the priesthood. Although Moses was not himself a priest, God gave him the honor of presiding over the consecration ceremony. And it was through these ceremonies that Aaron and his sons were set apart for specialized service to the Lord.

The Opening Ceremonies

The first acts in the consecration ceremony were the ritual washing, the putting on of the priestly clothing and vestments, and the anointing with oil (29:1–9). Being called and set apart for God's service is a solemn occasion. It began with the ritual washing—the cleansing (29:4). Such ritual washings or cleansings were common in Old Testament life and quite likely provide the rationale for the baptisms which John the Baptist performed. Here, too, we see symbolism that points toward Christian baptism as expressed by the great Apostle when he told the Roman Christians that "we are buried with him [Jesus Christ] by baptism into death: that like as Christ was raised up from the dead by the glory of the Father, even so we also should walk in newness of life" (Rom. 6:4).

Following the ceremonial washing or cleansing, the priests were to put on their special clothes in a formal ceremony (29:5–9). Finally, Moses was to take specially prepared oil, "and pour it upon his [Aaron's] head, and anoint him" (29:7).

The Sin Offering

These solemn acts of dedication were then followed by the "sin offering" (29:10–14). To twentieth-century Christians this seems like a strange ritual of worship. But to the ancient Hebrew each part of the offering carried special significance. First a bull was brought to Aaron and his sons. After all the priests had placed their hands on the bull's head, the animal was killed, and its blood, symbolic of life, was applied to the four horns of the Altar. Next, portions of the animal's body were roasted on the Altar, and the remainder of the carcass was taken outside the camp and burned.

In all of this we see that sin is not something that can be cleansed with water and soap. Instead, by the priests' placing their hands on the bull's head, their sins were transferred to the animal, which was then killed and destroyed by fire. In this act of sacrifice the sins of the priests were forgiven. For us, the offering becomes a symbol of Christ's mission as we envision sins being forgiven through the death of the sacrifice.

The Burnt Offering

The second sacrifice in this week-long ritual of consecration was called the burnt offering (29:15–18). For this offering a ram is brought to the priests, who all place their hands on the animal's head, again identifying themselves with the animal. And after the animal is killed the entire body is burned on the Altar. Burning the whole animal in this case, in contrast with burning only selected body parts in the sin offering, symbolized the complete giving of the priests to God. The upward movement of the smoke from the sacrifice symbolized the releasing of their lives to the Lord.

The Ram of Ordination

The final sacrifice was the peace offering (19:28) or ram of consecration (29:31). While both the sin and the burnt offerings were sacrificed on other ritual occasions, this particular offering was reserved only for the ordination of priests to God's service.

This time a ram was brought before the priests who again placed their hands upon the animal's head. After the ram was killed, a smear of blood was placed on each priest's right ear, thumb, and big toe, and then sprinkled over the priests' and their clothing. According to the ancient rabbis, the ear was touched with blood so it might hear the word of God, the hand was smeared with blood in order for it to perform priestly duties, and the foot was touched with blood so the priest would walk in the way of righteousness.

Next, various parts of the ram were "waved"— shaken back and forth—before the Lord, and then burned on the Altar. Finally, the remaining portions of the animal were cooked and eaten with the bread that was kept in a basket at the door of the Tabernacle (29:32). In this act of eating together in the presence of the Lord, the newly consecrated priests were symbolizing the communion that now existed between themselves and God.

The Daily Sacrifices

We are now told that in addition to the other sacrifices, a bull was to be offered as a continual atonement for sin during the entire seven day dedication period (29:36–37). But this ritual was not to end with the conclusion of the consecration ceremonies—it was to be continued every day, morning and evening. It was these daily sacrifices that solidified the covenant relationship between God and the people of Israel. The Exodus writer quotes God as saying, "And I will dwell among the children of Israel, and will be their God. And they shall know that I am the Lord their God, that brought them forth out of the land of Egypt, that I may dwell among them: I am the Lord their God" (29:45–46).

The thought of bloody animal sacrifices is difficult for modern Christians to appreciate. However, we must remember that Moses and the Hebrews were an ancient people who lived in a culture far different from ours. As time passed, the prophets expanded on the meaning of worship.

The prophet Micah, writing hundreds of years after Moses, stated that the Jews should not put such importance on animal sacrifice. Indeed, Micah said, "Wherewith shall I come before the Lord, and bow myself before the high God? shall I come before him with burnt offerings, with calves of a year old? Will the Lord be pleased with ten thousands of rams, or with ten thousands of rivers of oil? shall I give my firstborn for my transgression, the fruit of my body for the sin of my soul? He hath shewed thee, O man, what is good; and what doth the Lord require of thee, but to do justly, and to love mercy, and to walk humbly with thy God?" (Micah 6:6–8).

As Micah so insightfully observed, God isn't necessarily interested in material sacrifices from us. Rather, the truest worship of God and the most meaningful gift we can give Him is when we live our lives in such a way that we do create justice, treat others with kindness, and walk humbly with God. Our greatest offering is to live a Christlike life. This is why the Apostle Paul wrote, "I beseech you therefore, brethren, by the mercies of God, that ye present your bodies *a living sacrifice,* holy, acceptable unto God, which is your reasonable service" (Rom. 12:1, italics mine).

Final Instructions (30:1–38)

After the directions were given by God to Moses for the construction of their place of worship, for its major furnishings, for the priests' clothing and vestments, and for the service of consecration, He now goes on to give certain miscellaneous instructions concerning other Tabernacle furnishings and their worship.

The Altar of Incense

There's no particular significance to the fact that this Altar was not mentioned earlier when instructions were given for the Ark of the Covenant, the Table of Shewbread, and the Golden Lampstand—furnishings for the Tabernacle itself.

But now the Lord gives Moses instructions for building the Altar of Incense (30:1–10). This Altar, made of acacia wood and overlaid with gold, is to be eighteen inches square and thirty-six inches tall. It was to be situated in the first section of the Tabernacle just in front of the veil that divided the Holy of Holies from the Holy Place. From ancient times the smell of incense and the rising of its smoke upward symbolized the prayers of the people going up to God.

The Census Tax

Next the Lord gave Moses instructions for taking a census (30:11–16). The actual taking of this census is reported by the writer of the Book of Numbers (Chapter 1). When the count was taken, God told Moses that every Hebrew was to pay a half shekel tax that was to be used for the support and maintenance of the Tabernacle.

The Laver

The final piece of furniture that was to be a part of the Tabernacle complex was a bronze basin that was positioned in the courtyard between the Altar of

Burnt Offering and the door of the Tabernacle. After the priests had offered sacrifices on the Altar, they were to wash their hands and feet before entering the Tabernacle itself. To be ritually unclean in their worship was to invite death (30:20).

The Anointing Oil

The Lord then gave Moses precise instructions for the oil that was used to anoint people or objects (30:22–33). We may wonder at the amount of wordage and space given to this particular detail. But its importance begins to come through more clearly as we realize that in the ancient Near East, the anointing of a person or an object with oil had deep symbolic meaning. The anointing act identified those persons or objects as being set apart—consecrated—for special service to God. In addition, those persons anointed with the oil saw themselves as being empowered by God for service.

The Exodus writer tells us that the anointing oil was made of myrrh, cinnamon, cane, cassia, and pure olive oil. We might wonder where the former Hebrew slaves could possibly acquire the combinations of herbs, spices, and oil in the wilds of the Sinai desert. But it is safe to assume that these provisions could easily have been among those things the Egyptians impressed on their former neighbors before they left Egypt.

It is further made clear that this oil was never to be used in a nonsacramental way. Instead, it was for the anointing of the Tabernacle, its furnishings, the priests and the high priest.

Incense for the Altar

So that no detail essential to Tabernacle worship is omitted, the Lord then gave Moses instructions for the makeup of the incense that was to be burned on the Altar (30:34–38). Again attentive to detail the writer tells us the incense was a combination of stacte—evidently a sweet spice that may have come from the gum of the storax tree; onycha—made from certain kinds of mussel shells; galbanum—a resinous gum; and frankincense—obtained from tree bark that is native to Turkey and India. Frankincense was long-burning and gave a steady flame. It had a balsamlike odor and was quite expensive.

It is also likely these ingredients were brought with them from Egypt. The incense as with the anointing oil was restricted to use in worship.

While most Protestants in the Western world do not use incense in their worship, it was an important symbol of God's presence to the Hebrew worshipers. Even today, for many people there are other non-verbal means—sounds, for instance, a pipe organ's music, or a sung hymn—that help us feel and experience the nature and wonder of God.

Workman for the Task

I continue to be amazed at just how sensitive the Lord is to our needs and concerns. He had described at some length the intricate details for the astounding new place of worship for His people. Now He tells Moses that He has already prepared two men to handle the job of supervising the building of the Tabernacle and the furnishings. We're told their names were Bezaleel of the tribe of Judah and Aholiab of the tribe of Dan. Bezaleel was specified as the one in charge; his primary responsibility, however, was the metal, wood, and stone work. Aholiab was the specialist in textile fabrics (31:1–11).

We know very little more about either of these men. But they had been selected by God to use their unique gifts in fabricating a place of worship that in many ways is a symbolic model for us thousands of years later. Then and now God so often uses the "quiet people" to accomplish important jobs in the work of His new society. The activity of God through the church is most often carried on by little-known but Spirit-filled people who are committed witnesses to their faith.

There have been times when I've listened to a technically correct and skilled singer in concert but was completely unaffected by the artistry. There have been other times when a singer of lesser skills has moved me deeply because it was obvious that he or she was inspired by God. I believe this is the way it must have been with these two unknown Tabernacle builders in the Sinai desert. God was their inspiration. And it is this same God who will use us and our gifts in a redemptive way if we turn them over to Him.

God now concludes His special instructions for Moses with details about keeping the Sabbath (31:12–17). First, He said, "Ye shall keep the sabbath therefore; for it is holy unto you" (31:13–14). This reemphasis on the importance of the Sabbath might seem a bit unnecessary at this point. But it is possible that God wanted to remind His people that while the building of a place of worship was important, it must never take second place to actual worship and rest on the day set aside for that purpose.

I remember a friend telling me one time that while he believed in God, he didn't think it was necessary to go to church. He insisted that he could worship God just as well in the woods or by a lake or on the seashore. It is true, of course, that we can worship God anywhere. But the Christian faith is not to be lived in isolation. Rather, it is to be lived within the community of faith—we need each other as together we keep the Sabbath.

Keeping the Sabbath, both in rest and private prayer and with other believers, is essential for spiritual growth. We are not only to "witness" by being busily occupied in doing things, we are to "be witnesses." It is in *being* Christian that we become effective in the *doing.*

The Sabbath

The final words in our Scripture lesson are awesome, "And he [God] gave unto Moses, when he had made an end of communing with him upon mount Sinai, two tables of testimony, tables of stone, written with the finger of God" (31:18).

There can be no doubt as to the Author of what was written on the tables of stone. It was true that Moses cut and formed the stone tablets, but the contents were written "by the finger of God." The Law, the Ten Words, inscribed in stone on Mount Sinai have continued to be a profound basis of law and human behavior ever since.

The Giving of the Decalogue

As we've moved through the pages of this lesson, much of the description and the symbolism has probably seemed strange. We find it hard to identify

Its Meaning for Us

with a nomadic people camped in the desert at the foot of Mount Sinai some three thousand years ago. Their knowledge and understanding of God was quite different from ours in the late twentieth century.

Yet, there is much that we can learn from the way God dealt with our spiritual ancestors. This is especially true of His emphasis and detail on worship and service. In my study I have been profoundly impressed with the way God spelled out so carefully the pattern and materials for the Hebrews' place of worship. Nothing was left to chance. Every little detail was given, even to the ingredients for the anointing oil and the incense.

This tells me that our worship and our service for God must never be casual. Our acts and words of worship are never to be incidental. It is true, of course, that we don't worship in a portable Tabernacle or offer animal sacrifices. We live in a culture drastically different from the Hebrews in the Sinai peninsula and in Canaan. In Christ we have a New Covenant. But our needs for worship in preparation for service are not all that different!

Lord Father, Thank You for helping me to learn more about worship. Help me to worship You "in spirit and in truth." Touch me with Your Holy Spirit. AMEN.

WHAT THIS SCRIPTURE MEANS TO ME
Exodus 25—31

When I read the Scripture for this lesson, I thought of the old, worn adage, "First things first." Before God gave Moses instructions for building the Tabernacle, God asked for an offering from anyone who would give "willingly with his heart." I like that phrase and it reminds me of one line of a song that has stuck in my mind since I was a teenager when my family frequently listened to a record album produced by the Medical Mission Sisters. The songwriter, Sister Miriam Therese Winter, had added a catchy postscript onto words originally written by the Apostle Paul. In 2 Corinthians 9:7 he said, "God loveth a cheerful giver." The lighthearted singers continued, "Give it all you've got."

God may not ask us for precious metals and stones or for dyed linen and leather, but He still requires that we give with a willing heart.

My father was a pastor who had a vision for planting new churches. I well remember one such building project. When I was in junior high, we moved to a farm on the outer edge of suburbia. Next door in the center of the fruit orchard, I watched Father and the stone mason erect the church walls—one cinderblock at a time. Eventually, even I got in on the act; I grew quite proficient at mixing mortar, or "mud" as we called it.

As the small congregation had taken on such a large project, everyone felt the pinch of sacrificial giving—and maybe no one as much as my parents, who were willing to jump headfirst into this pioneer work. Even though they had two children in college and two still at home, they offered to cut their salary by more than half until the church got off the ground. I smile to think that that was the year the stereo turntable so frequently spun "God loves a cheerful giver."

God asks that we willingly give of our material wealth, but He also wants us to give of our talents and time. I like to think that my friend Mr. Gilbert was a modern-day Bezaleel, who was "filled with the spirit of God . . . and in all manner of workmanship" which he used for God's glory. Mr. Gilbert was the special parishioner who gave my parents that Medical Mission Sisters' record album. From nine to five during the week, he was an electronics engineer at General Dynamics. But that career was only a fraction of his life. He died when I was in college, but I will always remember him—at the church. Every Saturday and, it seemed, every evening, he was there in his green workclothes—wiring rooms or building chairs for children or oiling rafters.

He gave his talent to God's work, but he also willingly gave his time. I think that's the hardest thing for me to be cheerfully generous with. It's too easy to forget that each hour and each day which is mine to fill is a gift from God. It's too easy to forget the lines of 1 Chronicles 29:14, which I sing in every Sunday morning worship service: "All things come of thee, and of thine own have we given thee."

LESSON 6
Exodus 32

God Provides Forgiveness for His People

"If thou, Lord, shouldest mark iniquities, O Lord, who shall stand? But there is forgiveness with thee, that thou mayest be feared." AMEN.

She was obviously suffering from depression. As we continued to talk, her shoulders began to shake and she started sobbing. Overcome with a sense of guilt, this young woman was relentlessly punishing herself emotionally for a sinful action in her past which she could not forget and put behind her. Repeatedly she asked God for forgiveness. But like a barbed fish hook, the sin stayed lodged within her conscience.

What this woman desperately needed to realize is the truth of the theme of this thirty-second chapter of Exodus—our Scripture for this lesson. This truth is that God is always ready to forgive us if we turn to Him and follow His ways. Unfortunately, though God is ready to forgive, we are often unwilling to forgive ourselves or each other. The Exodus story brings hope to those who are "hooked" by guilt. It tells us that God is always able and ready to forgive.

We pick up now on the story line that we left with the last verse of Chapter 24, "And Moses went into

The Golden Calf (32:1–6)
Back to the Story

the midst of the cloud, and gat him up into the mount: And Moses was in the mount forty days and forty nights." The first words of our present Scripture lesson read, "And when the people saw that Moses delayed to come down out of the mount, the people gathered themselves together unto Aaron, and said unto him, Up, make us gods, which shall go before us; for as for this Moses, the man that brought us up out of the land of Egypt, we wot not what is become of him" (32:1).

Out of Sight, Out of Mind

For the Israelites it was out of sight, out of mind. Moses had been gone from the camp of Israel for a little over a month, and they were growing restless. Had Moses died? Had God forgotten them? As they pondered these questions, a terrible sense of uneasiness and anxiety seemed to hover over the camp like a dense fog.

They began to complain—something they were pretty good at since leaving Egypt. In spite of the fact that God had shown His greatness in the Egyptian plagues, had rolled back the waters of the sea so they could cross, and had provided food and drink and safety as they crossed the desert stretch to Sinai, they were ready to throw it all over and run, simply because Moses had been gone for a month or so.

"Make Us Gods"

In every crowd there are at least a few vocal troublemakers and malcontents. These apparently went into action at this point and whipped the crowd up demanding that Aaron make them gods they could see and visibly follow. At this stage of his life no one could accuse Aaron of bravery or strength of character, and there's certainly no indication in the story that Aaron tried to talk the people out of it. Instead, he takes immediate steps to comply and give the people what they want.

Obviously, there are details in the story that we don't have in these six verses, but we have enough to get the picture. Aaron tells the people to bring him their gold earrings and from these he cast a "molten calf" (32:2–4). Other translations better convey the meaning of the Hebrew word in referring to it as a bull or bull calf. In the ancient Near East, the depiction of a god as a bull was widespread. The bull was a symbol of strength, vitality, fertility, and lordship.

We are next told that Aaron built an altar before the bull-god. There they worshiped and offered sacrifices—a blatant violation of the law that they were to worship no god but God—Yahweh. They were not only guilty of breaking their covenant with God, they had formed a god that could be grasped, managed, and manipulated—a god made out of their own jewelry and with their own hands.

In our twentieth-century Christian sophistication it is easy for us to ridicule their primitive ways. And while we don't bow down before or pray to golden bulls, we are often guilty of paying homage to gods we can see and feel. In our urge to feel secure, we often attempt to capture God's presence in visible things—church buildings, creeds, the Bible, a prayer book, clergy persons.

It is just as true now as it was three thousand years ago that God cannot be contained. We can't build a fence around Him. Instead, we must accept the fact that we will have moments when God will seem absent or far away. But rather than panic and form our own idolatrous and controllable image of God, we must instead simply wait. God will "return" and fill us with His Spirit. Both the Psalmist and the Wisdom writers understood this when they wrote, "Wait on the Lord: be of good courage, and he shall strengthen thine heart" (Psa. 27:14), and "Wait on the Lord, and he shall save thee" (Prov. 20:22).

Centuries later the prophet Isaiah was in exile and often felt that God had deserted him. Yet in his wisdom he knew that his awareness of God would return. In writing to his fellow exiles he said, "Why sayest thou, O Jacob, and speakest, O Israel, My way is hid from the Lord, and my judgment is passed over from my God? . . . But they that wait upon the Lord shall renew their strength; they shall mount up with wings as eagles; they shall run, and not be weary; and they shall walk, and not faint" (Isa. 40:27, 31).

When it seems to us that God is secluded on some distant mountaintop and we are stuck down in the hot, dry desert, we aren't to panic or turn to false

God Cannot Be Contained

141

gods. Instead, we are to be patient, for our awareness of God's presence will return. Once again we will "mount up with wings as eagles."

Elijah's Experience

In another part of our Old Testament there is a marvelous story about Elijah, God's prophet. The writer of 1 Kings (Chapters 18 and 19) tells us about Elijah's wonderful victory over the prophets of Baal on Mount Carmel. But when Queen Jezebel heard about it, she was furious and, in a fit of anger, warned the prophet that he would be dead in twenty-four

Pictured here is the Plain of Rest the traditional site of the Hebrews' camp at the base of Mount Sinai. This is also thought to be the setting for the golden bull-calf episode.

hours. She was humiliated because Elijah had won out over her prophets, and she swore vengeance.

In the face of the queen's violent anger, Elijah's blood turned to water. In spite of past victories he was sure God had forgotten him, so he turned and ran—all the way south from central Palestine to the southern desert of the Negev. There, alone, depressed, without food and water, and wanting to die, Elijah was without hope. But then we read that God sent an angel to care for him. And in the cave on Mount Horeb a gentle and patient God first paraded His might before the prophet and then spoke to him out of the stillness and silence, assuring him that he had not been forgotten (1 Kings 19:9–18).

Footprints in the Sand

There is a wonderful modern-day parable that comes to us from an unknown source that illustrates vividly the Lord's presence with us even though we may think He is distant and we can't feel His presence. It is the story of a man who had a dream one night in which he was walking with the Lord on the seashore. As they walked along, the man realized that a sequence of scenes from his own life was appearing in the sky. Pictured above him were the important events of his life. After viewing the last scene the man looked behind him and there stretched out in the distance he saw two sets of footprints. But every once in a while only one set could be seen.

As he reflected on this strange sight, he realized that when a difficult and particularly needy time in his life had been pictured in the sky, just one set of footprints appeared in the sand. After reflecting on the phenomenon for a time, he turned to the Lord and said, "You told me when I turned my life over to You that if I would walk with You, You would always be with me. Why did You leave me alone in my times of greatest need?"

The Lord answered, "I didn't leave you. When you saw only one set of footprints, it was then that I was carrying you."

A God of Forgiveness (32:7–14)

The Lord's Indignation

In the meantime, back up on the mountain, God, of course, knew what was going on, "And the Lord said unto Moses, Go, get thee down; for thy people, which thou broughtest out of the land of Egypt, have corrupted themselves" (32:7). He then went on to tell Moses about the bull idol. Then God said, "I have seen this people, and, behold, it is a stiffnecked [stubborn, headstrong] people: Now therefore let me alone, that my wrath may wax hot against them, and that I may consume them: and I will make of thee a great nation" (32:9–10).

Moses' Prayer and God's Response

When Moses realized that God intended to destroy the Hebrews because of their sin and begin again with Moses as the father of a new nation, he began immediately to intercede for his people (32:11–13). Begging God to remember His covenant with His people and to understand the stress of the journey that had brought them to this sin, Moses asked God to forgive them. In response to Moses' prayer the Exodus writer tells us that "the Lord repented of the evil which he thought to do unto his people" (32:14).

What does it mean for the Lord "to repent"? This in no way means that God is capable of evil. Rather, the Hebrew word, *nacham,* which has been translated "repent," can best be defined as "to change one's mind." This simply means that when God saw and heard the grief in Moses' face and voice over the possible destruction of his people, He was moved to compassion and to forgiveness.

In this ancient understanding of God, we see one of the primary attributes of God displayed. Our God is not one who is emotionally removed from His people. He doesn't have an "I could care less" attitude. Rather, He is passionately in relationship with us and feels keenly the pain of our sinful action. When we ask to be forgiven, we are always pardoned.

Let us not forget the importance, however, of Moses' prayer of intercession for his people. It was Moses' prayers, not theirs, that resulted in eventual reconciliation.

I know a young man who in earlier days was extremely wild and rebellious. We knew him to be a real rounder. He was a source of grave concern to his godly parents. And even though they didn't seem to have any influence on him, they continued to pray faithfully for their son. As time passed, there was indication that this man was going through a spiritual struggle. Finally, a series of painful events brought him to the place where he asked God for forgiveness. As a result of his conversion, his life was changed radically.

I'm convinced that one of the major causes for this man's conversion was the faithful and urgent prayers of his mother and father. Prayer does make a difference today, just as it did for Moses.

Following the dramatic exchange between Moses and God high up on Sinai's peak, Moses headed down the mountain, with the two stone tablets in his hands. He was evidently joined by Joshua on the lower slopes, and the two walked on down together out of the foothills. As they got close to the camp, they heard a loud commotion which Joshua thought was the sound of battle (32:15, 17–18). But God had warned Moses about what was going on, so he recognized the noise for what it was.

An Abuse of Leadership (32:15–24)
Moses Takes Charge

As they came to the camp, Moses was holding firmly to the two stone tablets on which the finger of God had etched the Ten Commandments. The words on these two tablets were to be the guidelines by which the Hebrews lived. But as Moses saw firsthand the sickening sight of his people worshiping the gold bull, he was filled with rage. And there, in the sight of his people, he threw the tablets to the ground where they broke into pieces—a tragic symbol that the Hebrews had broken their covenant promise.

In colorful language the Exodus writer shows us Moses' next actions, "And he took the calf which they had made, and burnt it in the fire, and ground it to powder, and strawed [sprinkled] it upon the water, and made the children of Israel drink of it" (32:20). In doing this Moses gave his people an object lesson they would long remember—the gold bull had no status or power as a god.

A Colorful Object Lesson

145

Moses Confronts Aaron

With the disappearance of the god made with human hands, Moses turned on his brother Aaron whom he had left in charge. In outrage Moses demanded to know how this sin could have been allowed to happen (32:21).

A frightened and flustered Aaron passed the buck to his fellow Hebrews, and then made one of the silliest statements in the whole story. With a straight face, I suppose, Aaron told Moses that he just threw the gold into the fire "and there came out this calf" (32:24). He refused to accept responsibility for his actions.

Abuse of responsibility is one of the great tragedies in our Christian world. One way or another, we are all leaders—we are people with influence in our own worlds. One of the characteristics of a true leader is the ability to withstand popular pressure to go against what we know to be right. Our role is not meant to be adversarial, yet we are not to compromise what we believe and understand to be the Lord's leading.

The result of irresponsibility explodes into reality as Moses, in this case, tells Aaron that he had caused the Hebrews to sin. Had Aaron held firm and refused to compromise, the Hebrews would not have had to suffer for their sin the way they did.

As Christian leaders, the commission to witness and be witnesses carries a heavy load of responsibility for all of us. We aren't called, I believe, to a razzle-dazzle, exhibitionist kind of faith in which we attempt to outdo and upstage one another with pious theatrics. Instead we are called to live out daily an authentic faith that exemplifies the spirit of the simple Carpenter of Nazareth who asked that His disciples not reveal who He was as he went about quietly caring for the needs of people in trouble. In the same way our worship is to be focused on the true God and not on the false gods of size or popularity or materialism in any of its deadly forms.

A Provocative Scene (32:25–29)

As we've seen, Moses was aroused to vigorous anger over the depravity of his people. It is also possible that a rebellion of sorts had arisen among some of the people who had come to resent Moses' authority. The disrespectful wording in 32:1—as for this fellow Moses, we don't know what's happened to him—has the ring of rebellion.

The Exodus writer doesn't say that Moses got any word from the Lord, but we next see him standing at a prominent place in the camp and rallying the faithful to the Lord's side. That day, those who were rebellious and unfaithful met their fate by the edge of a sword. "There fell of the people that day about three thousand men" (32:28).

The making and worshiping of the bull-calf at the foot of the mountain of God was tragic heresy, and heresy has always, through all history, created havoc and a spirit of rebellion among the people of God.

This idea of bull worship was a throwback to their Mesopotamian background and was apparently practiced in Ur by the time of Abraham. Then, too, they had been exposed to it in Egypt. So it appears the stain of bull worship had remained with them, and it continued to be a recurring heresy until the Hebrews returned from exile in Babylon centuries later.

The Meaning for Us of the Bull-Calf Episode

This whole strange scene seems unreal to us as we attempt to live the Christian life in our late twentieth-century world. Yet, as the Apostle Paul wrote to his young friend Timothy, all Scripture is helpful as a guide "for reproof, for correction, for instruction in righteousness" (2 Tim. 3:16).

There are many lessons we can learn from this event, but to me there are some that stand out above the others.

1. God is always with us whether we "feel" His presence or not. We all have moments when God doesn't seem to be there at all or is far away. Then, too, there are those times when we don't "feel" the support of other Christians. This was the mood of the Hebrews when Moses was on the mountain—out of sight and with no word from him for forty days.

2. Idolatry of any kind and description is a deadly enemy to our faith. It can take many different and subtle forms, but put simply, anything, irrespective

of how good and worthwhile it may be, that replaces God in our lives is sin.

3. Moses' prayer that God would spare his people even though they were guilty of the grossest sin was answered, and God's mercy was experienced by all of the people. It was Moses' prayers that made the difference. We are to be a people of prayer because prayer does change things.

4. To avoid the subtleties of being led astray into idol worship of any kind or falling for any of the distortions of the Christian faith, we are to be avid students of the Word of God and of the teachings of the Church in fellowship with other believers. It is in earnest and open-minded study that the Spirit of God shows us truth.

The Price of Sin (32:30–35)
Moses Stands in the Gap

As the tragic scene that has occupied our attention in this lesson draws to a close, we are given a remarkable picture of Moses as a mighty man of faith who cares deeply about his people. He reminds them they have sinned greatly against their God, but he tells them now that he is going back up the mountain in an effort to "make an atonement for your sin" (32:30).

Next, the Exodus writer shares with us the conversation that went on between Moses and God on the slopes of Sinai, "Oh, this people have sinned a great sin, and have made them gods of gold. Yet now, if thou wilt forgive their sin—; and if not, blot me, I pray thee, out of thy book which thou hast written" (32:31–32). Amazing! Moses was willing for God to take his life as an atoning sacrifice for the sin of his people, if that was the only way.

God Forgives But Consequences Remain

Refusing to punish Moses for the sins of his people, God said that each person was responsible for his or her sins (32:33). Then the Lord told Moses that the people should continue on toward the Promised Land, but their sin of idolatry would have long-lasting consequences.

It is true, of course, that God forgives us for our sins. But the consequences of our sins may be felt for a long time. I have a friend who during his high school years would frequently get drunk at weekend parties. One night while racing home after getting drunk at one of those parties, he lost control of his car and collided with a tree. His injuries were severe, and his right arm had to be amputated.

Even though God had long ago forgiven him for his sin, he is "plagued" by his past actions every day of his life. We who believe in the grace of God and the forgiveness of sin must never be lured into taking lightly the results of sin. To break any one of the commandments of God is to invite lifelong consequences.

As we look back over this lesson, the amazing light that shines through brightly is the mercy and grace of God. Though our Lord is keenly pained by our sins, He is always ready to forgive when we ask. And in spite of the consequences of our actions, He is faithful to lead each of us on toward our individual Promised Lands.

Paul, an Example for Us

There can be no doubt but that Saul of Tarsus—later Paul the Apostle—knew what it meant to sin against God. He had, undoubtedly, been an active participant of the mob who had stoned Stephen to death because of his Christian testimony (Acts 7:58). And he had been a vigorous persecutor of the early Christian believers. But there can be no doubt but that after the Damascus Road experience that resulted in his conversion to Christ, he was forgiven for all past sins.

Yet we have clues in certain of Paul's later words that he was keenly aware of his past, and while we have no way of knowing, it is quite possible that in the darkness of the night hours, more than once he saw Stephen's face as he died. Though Paul was forgiven, the consequences of his past were doubtless with him one way or another throughout the rest of his life. But, convinced of the love and grace of God, Paul didn't let guilt destroy him.

In writing to the Roman Christians Paul once said that everybody has sinned and fallen short of God's glory, yet in spite of that we are made righteous through God's grace (Rom. 3:23–24). But in this sordid scene we've just studied we've seen God's mercy and forgiveness at work. The Good News throughout all of the Old and New Testament is that God forgives, and we can begin over again. Because, as Paul wrote, if anyone is "in Christ, *he is a new creature: old things are passed away; behold, all things are become new* (2 Cor. 5:17, italics mine).

Father God, Thank You for making me brand new—You've redeemed my past, even the times when I've sinned, suffered hurt or persecution, neglect, or abuse. Thank You for working all of my life after the counsel of Your will. AMEN.

WHAT THIS SCRIPTURE MEANS TO ME
Exodus 32

My brother, who teaches at a Christian college, recently walked into the school cafeteria and joined a circle of students who were enumerating their parents' pharisaical sins. One young man listened to all the accusations and then spoke up, "Well, my parents *aren't* hypocrites." He proceeded to tell an incident that had changed his life.

For a while, in high school, he had hung out with "the wrong crowd," and one weekend night he had stayed out way past his curfew. In the middle of the night he had quietly snuck in the house, hoping he wouldn't be heard, only discovered after dawn—soundly asleep in his bed. His plan worked; his parents didn't hear him, at least not until after he had heard them. As he tiptoed down the hall toward the bedrooms, he stopped and listened. His mother and father were awake and praying for their son's safety and well-being. Like Moses, who pleaded that God temper His anger, this mother and father poured out their hearts, interceding on behalf of their wayward son. He saw their earnestness and decided that he wanted to know their God.

The heart-wrenching concern of God's faithful people does produce results!

As I read this golden calf story in Exodus, I notice that it doesn't end with Moses' mediating prayer. After he sees the idol and understands why God is so angry, Moses prays again, this time going so far as to offer himself as a sacrifice for the people he has come to love.

In his autobiographical love story, *A Severe Mercy,* Sheldon Vanauken tells how, after they had been happily married for several years, his wife, Davy, became a Christian. Like Moses, who offered to take the people's sin upon himself, Davy told God she was willing to die if her death would be the means by which Sheldon's soul would "be fulfilled." Of course, we don't know all the whys and wherefores of God's acts, but within eighteen months of Davy's prayer, she died of a rare disease. And yes, it seems her death prompted Sheldon to put his life in God's hands.

That kind of selfless, sacrificial love is at the center of the Christian faith. The Apostle Paul mentions it in Romans 5:7–8: "Scarcely for a righteous man will one die. . . . But God commendeth his love toward us, in that, while we were yet sinners, Christ died for us."

Although Moses was willing, God did not allow him to charge the people's sin to his own account. That substitutionary sacrifice was to be reserved for God Himself. In the nineteenth century, Cecil Alexander wrote the poem, "There Is a Green Hill Far Away," the fourth verse of which succinctly describes Christ's crucifixion, God's provision for our forgiveness, and a response that we can make:

There was no other good enough
To pay the price of sin;
He only could unlock the gate
Of heaven and let us in.
Oh, dearly, dearly has He loved,
And we must love Him, too;
And trust in His redeeming blood,
And try His works to do.

Moses loved his people; the student's parents loved him; Davy loved Sheldon—all because they loved God who first loved them. It sounds like a circle that never ends—a merry-go-round of love on which I want to ride.

LESSON 7
Exodus 33–34

God Provides His Presence for His People

Abba Father, Thank You for being present in all the circumstances of my life. You're with me not only in times of prayer and meditation, but in times of frustration, turmoil, pressure. Lord, help me to tap into Your presence and power each moment of the day. AMEN.

Even though, as we will see shortly, the people of Israel were not ready to leave the Sinai region quite yet, our Scripture lesson opens with God reaffirming the promise He had made to Abraham almost five hundred years before at Shechem. Here the Lord tells Moses that they are to leave Sinai and head north for that land which He had promised to "Abraham, to Isaac, and to Jacob" (33:1).

The Lord then assures Moses that an angel will travel with them, "and I will drive out the Canaanite, the Amorite, and the Hittite, and the Perizzite, the Hivite, and the Jebusite" (33:2). These are the ancient tribes that occupied various places in the Land of Promise.

The Canaanites referred to here were descendants of Canaan, the grandson of Noah, who occupied part of the Jordan Valley and a stretch of land along the seashore. They were located in the lowlands. By con-

Sin Separates (33:1–6)
Traveling Instructions

trast, the Amorites occupied the mountainous areas from west of the Dead Sea to the Hebron region. At the time of Abraham, there were Hittites in the Hebron area—it was from one of them that Abraham acquired a family burial cave. But the Hittites along with the Hivites lived mostly in northern and western Palestine. The Perizzites and the Jebusites were located in the central and southern sections of Canaan, with the Jebusites occupying that area later known as Jerusalem.

In other words, in specifying those tribes that would be conquered, the Lord was reaffirming that the entire land of Promise was theirs to take—a land "flowing with milk and honey," a prosperous and fertile country. For Moses and the children of Israel, camped as they were in the parched Sinai desert, their new homeland must have sounded like a paradise.

The Scope of God's Promise

Once again, we can't help but marvel at the detail given us here. While the Exodus writer's purpose isn't to give a history record as such, he does want his readers to understand, I believe, that when God promises something, as he did to Abraham, Isaac, and Jacob—and now to Moses—He intends to keep His promise. God's promises to *us* are just as inclusive and certain as they were to His chosen people thousands of years ago.

We can count on God—and what a God He is! Just while writing this I heard the report about the space vehicle that was launched by our space people ten years ago. It has traveled two billion miles and has sent back pictures of planets our scientists had never seen before in the same way. Now, in its eleventh year, this spaceship is continuing on its way to other planets even further out into the distant reaches of the universe.

Never by the wildest stretch of his imagination could the Psalmist have pictured the immensity of God's world, yet we are indebted to him for these words; "For as the heaven is high above the earth, so great is his mercy [love] toward them that fear him" (Psa. 103:11). And in another place the Psalmist wrote, "I will praise thee, O Lord, among the people:

I will sing unto thee among the nations. For thy mercy [unfailing love] is great unto the heavens [as wide as the heavens], and thy truth unto the clouds [the skies]" (Psa. 57:9–10).

It was this God who talked with Moses on Mount Sinai. And it is this God who is with you and me during our twenty-four-hour days and seven-day weeks!

An Angel but Not the Lord Would Be With Them

In verse 2 the Lord told Moses He would send an angel with the Israelites when they entered Canaan. Now He adds, "for I will not go up in the midst of thee" (33:3). God Himself was with them at Sinai. But He would not be with them in the same way as they moved on. He would be with them in a spiritual sense, but not in a personal way. God reminds them they are a "stiffnecked"—stubborn—people, and His holiness would "consume" them. When the people heard this disturbing news they went into mourning and removed their jewelry as an outward sign of remorse (33:4–6).

I was talking recently with a young man who had not become a Christian until after his graduation from college. The change in his life was quite radical, and he enjoyed an extremely warm and intimate relationship with God. He worded it this way, "God and I talked all the time. He was close by."

But then, he told me, that in recent months he had been going through some very difficult times and was feeling a great deal of stress. His father had died, he had changed jobs and moved to a different city, and he was experiencing some rather difficult marital adjustments. Along with all of that, he was maturing in his faith and had begun to wonder about some of his earlier attitudes and ideas. Now, in the midst of all of this trauma, he was feeling that God had removed His presence from him. As the "high" of his conversion experience and his new-found faith became more distant in his past, God no longer seemed right there at his fingertips. And he even wondered if God wasn't punishing him for something.

I assured this young man that what he was going through was natural, and that he could be utterly confident that God had not forsaken him and certainly wasn't punishing him.

Mountain Peaks and Valleys

We've all had spiritual peak experiences when we've felt that we were on a mountaintop with the Lord. At such times we've probably felt the same emotions as Peter, James, and John when they were with Jesus on the Mount of Transfiguration. We'd like to "build three tabernacles" so we could stay there permanently. But that's not the way life works. We have to go down into the valley of life, the ordinary and nitty-gritty, to be with people and respond to their needs.

Down in our "life valleys" we experience those times when God seems distant. Often these moments come during times of emotional crisis when our feelings are raw or numb. Then, too, as with the Hebrews, we may have periods when we don't experience spiritual intimacy because of unconfessed sin or unresolved guilt. But for whatever reason, when God seems far away, it is important to remember that "feelings" cannot always be trusted. These are times when we are to hold steady and in faith claim God's promise not to leave us. The writer of the Book of Hebrews (13:5) reminds his readers of the assurance Moses gave the Hebrews on the eve of his death just before they moved across Jordan into The Promised Land. "Be strong and of good courage, fear not, nor be afraid of them: for the Lord thy God, he it is that doth go with thee; he will not fail thee, nor forsake thee" (Deut. 31:6). It is this kind of confident faith and hope that will carry us through to ever greater moments with God.

God Restores His Presence (33:7–23)
The Tent of Meeting

The scene shifts now as the Exodus writer says that "Moses took the tabernacle, and pitched it without the camp, afar off from the camp, and called it the Tabernacle of the congregation. And it came to pass, that every one which sought the Lord went out unto the tabernacle of the congregation, which was without the camp" (33:7).

The wording here should not cause us to confuse this tent with the Tabernacle that was described for us in Exodus 25–31. That portable dwelling place of the Lord had not been built yet. The tabernacle or tent referred to in our lesson now was a much simpler structure. In other translations this structure is referred to as The Tent of Meeting or The Tent of the Presence.

Another difference that sets this tent or tabernacle apart from the one that was to be the portable dwelling place for the Lord is that this one was outside the camp. The Tabernacle yet to be built was to be right in the middle of the camp.

Remember, the Hebrews had not yet moved camp. They were still at the foot of the mountain. It was up on the mountain that God and Moses had talked. But now, this Tent of Meeting, pitched just outside the camp, was also to be a meeting place between Moses and God.

Once again the Exodus writer treats us to an awesome sight, "And it came to pass, as Moses entered into the tabernacle [The Tent of Meeting], the cloudy pillar descended, and stood at the door of the tabernacle, *and the Lord talked with Moses.* And all the people saw the cloudy pillar stand at the tabernacle door: and all the people rose up and worshipped, every man in his tent door" (33:9–10, italics mine).

Next, we read that inside the Tent of Meeting the "Lord spake unto Moses face to face, as a man speaketh unto his friend" (33:11). In the verses that follow we hear Moses pleading with the Lord not to stay at a distance from His people (33:13–16). Moses knew that without God in their midst the Hebrews were helpless.

The Friend of God

Once again, Moses' persistence in prayer brought forth a favorable response from the Lord as He said, *"My presence shall go with thee,* and I will give thee rest" (33:14, italics mine). In these words we have another marvelous proof of God's mercy and grace in the Old Testament setting. Moved by human need and Moses' prayer, God promises to be with His people.

When Moses heard this good news, he had an overwhelming desire to know God even better. "I beseech thee," he boldly asked, "shew me thy glory" (33:17–18). To see the "glory of God" would be to see His character in full. This was more than God was willing to do—for Moses' sake. No one can see God and live (33:20). But He tells Moses he can get a partial glimpse of His glory and will see His goodness as a gracious and merciful God. Moses will be protected and covered in a crack in the mountain. While he will not see the Lord's face, he will get a glimpse of His character—God's "back parts" (33:19–23).

Men and women of all time have longed to see clearly God's glory and essence. But as with Moses, no person can ever see His "face." The Apostle Paul, like Moses, hungered to know God more fully. But he was allowed only a faint glimpse. Reflecting on this limited vision, Paul wrote, "For now we see through a glass, darkly; but then face to face: now I know in part; but then shall I know even as also I am known" (1 Cor. 13:12).

What marvelous Good News! While we make our way through the ordinary routines as well as the times of trouble that fill our lives, we have the assurance of God's presence—He is with us through His Spirit. But the time is coming when *we shall see His glory!*

The Covenant Restored (34:1–28)
Two New Stone Tablets

As Moses prepared to leave the Tent of Meeting, the Lord gave him a new set of instructions, "Hew thee two tables of stone like unto the first: and I will write upon these tables the words that were in the first tables, which thou brakest. And be ready in the morning, and come up in the morning unto mount Sinai, and present thyself there to me in the top of the mount" (34:1–2).

Moses is obedient to God's instructions as he prepares two more tables of stone. The next morning, with stone tablets in hand, Moses once again climbs the heights of Sinai. Then we read that the "Lord descended in a cloud," and it was then that Moses received his limited glimpse of God, accompanied by the awesome and majestic words, "The Lord, The Lord God, *merciful and gracious, longsuffering, and abundant in goodness and truth"* (34:6). What a powerful and awe-inspiring description of God!

Merciful and Gracious, Patient and Good

The two descriptive words, "merciful" and "gracious," speak of a God who understands our weaknesses as human beings. He is also a God who acts out of profound kindness. The Apostle Paul expressed this well when he wrote, "But God commendeth his love toward us, in that, while we were yet sinners, Christ died for us" (Rom. 5:8). Here we have a description of God's grace—His unmerited favor. He is a God who is steadfast—can be counted on—and is completely trustworthy.

The same God who met Moses that day on the mountain is the God who "so loved the world, that he gave his only begotten Son, that whosoever believeth in him should not perish, but have everlasting life" (John 3:16). Is it any wonder then that we read, "Moses made haste, and bowed his head toward the earth," and as he worshiped, prayed once again that the Lord would pardon the stubborn Hebrews (34:8–9).

The Covenant

Once again Moses' prayer is answered as God says, "Behold I make a covenant: before all thy people I will do marvels, such as have not been done in all the earth, nor in any nation: and all the people among which thou art shall see the work of the Lord: for it is a terrible [fearful] thing that I will do with thee" (34:10).

In this introduction to the covenant God makes it plain that He will reveal Himself to the whole world through the Hebrew people. God will, through His people, do "marvels" that all nations will recognize as "the work of the Lord."

Then, in anticipation of the future time when the Hebrews would emerge from the desert and enter Canaan, God warns them not to be influenced by the pagan worship of the people around them and not to intermarry with them (34:11–17). And as a grim reminder of their vulnerability, God concludes His warning by saying, "Thou shalt make thee no molten gods."

Next, God gave Moses the conditions of the covenant—the commandments they are to keep. Essentially, the conditions are the same as were given before, especially the Sabbath and God's claim on every firstborn child and animal. In addition provisions are given for keeping the Feast of Weeks (Pentecost), the

The old covenant was associated with the tablets of stone that Moses carried down from the peak of Mount Sinai. Shown above is a view of the traditional peak of the mountain and the desolate terrain that was home to the Israelites at that time.

Feast of Ingathering (Tabernacles), the Feast of Unleavened Bread, and the Passover (34:18, 22, 23, 25).

The Exodus writer now tells us that Moses remained on the mountain *"with the Lord* forty days and forty nights; he did neither eat bread, nor drink water" (34:28). Then he came down the mountain with the inscribed tables of stone.

A Glowing Countenance (34:29–35)

When Moses arrived back in camp, he was a changed man—"his face shone" and the people were "afraid to come nigh him" (34:29–30). Being with

God had given him a new look—he came to literally reflect the glory of God. We need to understand that the glow on Moses' face wasn't due to any native spiritual quality he possessed. Rather, it was the power, glory, and nature of God radiating through him.

There have been times in the course of my ministry that I have been asked by married couples to take them through a redeclaration of their wedding vows. As a rule such requests are made when a couple has lived together for a long time, and they now more fully understand what those vows mean than when they took them the first time. As their vows are taken a second time, their voices have a ring of authenticity and their faces shine more brightly than the first time around.

In a similar way there come moments to many of us when we want to renew our vows to God and rededicate our lives to Him. As the years have passed since our first experience, we have come to better understand what it means to live for the Lord. So, our fresh commitment—a renewal of our first covenant—is much more profound and brilliant than at first.

Now, I've never seen a person's face radiating a glow that was so bright that I needed a veil to protect my eyes as did the Israelites. However, I have, as I'm sure you have, been around people who vividly radiated the love and peace of God on their faces and in their attitudes and actions. Like Moses, they are so spiritually attuned to the Spirit of God that His Spirit shines through them.

In the early part of this lesson I told the story about a young man who was very concerned because he no longer seemed to feel the presence of God in his life. Now, here's the good news. Several weeks after we talked he walked into my office just glowing—grinning from ear to ear. He told me that one day when he was reading his Bible, without warning tears came to his eyes. He felt the presence of God very near. Emotionally, he had broken through his numbness to discover that God had been there all the time. The message of God's Word is clear—for those who trust Him, God is there!

A later Psalmist picked up on this part of the Moses story and wrote:

> He made his ways known unto Moses,
>   his acts unto the children of Israel.
> The Lord is merciful and gracious,
>   slow to anger, and plenteous in mercy.
> He will not always chide:
>   neither will he keep his anger for ever.
> He hath not dealt with us after our sins;
>   nor rewarded us according to our iniquities.
> For as the heaven is high above the earth,
>   so great is his mercy toward them that fear him.
> As far as the east is from the west,
>   so far hath he removed our transgressions from us.

(Psa. 103:7–12)

Blessed Assurance! Jesus is mine. Oh, what a foretaste of glory divine! Heir of salvation, purchase of God; born of His Spirit, washed in His blood. AMEN.

WHAT THIS SCRIPTURE MEANS TO ME
Exodus 33—34

For years I've been fascinated by the importance of names—not their literal meanings as much as their very existence. Our names remind us of who we are. They identify us to other people. In a mysterious way, they give us a sense of personal value.

A year ago I moved from New Jersey to Virginia, and immediately I started attending a large, active church. Although I never felt at home there, I stayed for eight months before trying a smaller church closer to my home. Within a month I knew that I would settle into this second congregation. I tried to analyze what this church had done that the first hadn't, and one thing immediately overshadowed any other thoughts: the pastor and people in the small neighborhood church remembered my name. That personal touch drew me to them.

In her book *The Summer of the Great-Grandmother,* Madeleine L'Engle noted that "to the ancient Hebrew the ultimate hell consisted in being forgotten, erased from the memory of family and tribe, from the memory of God."* Having lived alone for years, I've experienced that terror which comes from feeling as if I've been forgotten, erased from people's memory. But when those ill-founded fears start to creep into my mind, I remind myself that God, who knew Moses by name (Exodus 33:12, 17), knows and remembers the identity of *all* His children. Jesus clearly says this in John 10:3, where He refers to Himself as the Shepherd: His "sheep hear his voice: and he calleth his own sheep by name." I find great comfort in the fact that I have a God who knows me intimately.

As personal as my relationship to God is, I know that He knows me better than I know Him. Like Moses, I yearn for that face-to-face encounter with God that will be mine only when I cross the bar between earth and heaven, when I put on my clothes of immortality. Until that time, I must rest in the hope expressed by the Apostle Paul in 1 Corinthians 13:12: "For now we see through a glass, darkly; but then face to face: now I know in part; but then shall I know even as also I am known." Until that time, I must continue to seek His face through His Word and through His creation.

Even though God did not show Moses His face, God revealed His long name, His personal identity, His character: "The Lord God, merciful and gracious, longsuffering, and abundant in goodness and truth . . . forgiving,"

*Madeleine L'Engle, *The Summer of the Great-Grandmother* (New York: Farrar, Straus and Giroux), 1974.

and "Jealous" (34:6–7, 14). When Moses came down off the mountain there was no doubt in the people's minds that Moses had been in the Lord's presence. They could see it in him; his face shone.

Last summer I visited an old fashioned Methodist camp meeting where I met Esther, an elderly widow whose countenance revealed her personal relationship with God. There was nothing beautiful about Esther that made her stand out in a crowd. In fact, time had taken its toll on her physical body. She had never been more than five feet tall, but in her old age she'd shriveled and shrunk by two inches. Yet Esther immediately caught my eye. Her face radiated the joy of her salvation. Her smile was constant yet genuine, and it seemed to give an upward turn to every line in her gnarled face.

I left Esther's presence wishing her radiant face were my own. Well, I *could* do without the wrinkles. But the joy—I wanted it to shine as a testimony to my relationship with God.

LESSON 8
Exodus 35–40

God Provides Direction for His People

Father, Thank You for Your direction. You haven't left me to wander and wonder, to uncertainty and indecision. Thank You for leading me after Your own counsel. AMEN.

As we come to this final lesson in the drama in the Book of Exodus, we find the Hebrews still camped at the foot of Mount Sinai in the desert. Moses has come down Mount Sinai for the last time. The covenant between God and His people has been restored, and they now have the Law inscribed by God on the two tablets of stone. There is one thing yet to do before they break camp and move north toward the Land of Promise—the building of the Tabernacle.

You will recall our detailed study in Lesson 5 in which the Lord laid out the pattern for the building of His portable place of worship. In Chapters 25–31 the Lord, leaving nothing to chance, gave Moses every detail concerning the layout, structure, source materials, and furnishings for the Tabernacle. At the same time, the Lord gave Moses instructions on how the high priest and the priests should dress and how the sacrificial rituals of worship were to be handled.

Now, in our Scripture for this lesson we have

Building the Tabernacle (35:1–40:38)

Moses and the Hebrews actually doing what God had earlier told them to do. First, they were given the pattern right down to the smallest detail. Now, the pattern takes shape.

Why did the writer of Exodus devote ten chapters out of forty to the Tabernacle, its priestly attendants, and certain aspects of its use in worship? Why do we have five chapters containing God's instructions and then another almost identical five chapters devoted to the execution of the original instructions?

First, I believe this was done against the backdrop of the Hebrews' disobedience to God in breaking the covenant through worship of the bull-calf. When God gave the first instructions for building the Tabernacle, it was before the Hebrews had broken the covenant with their sin. But then as we saw in the last lesson, the people's repentance, along with Moses' intercession on their behalf, led to forgiveness and a renewal of the covenant. To symbolize and emphasize this renewal and the presence of God dwelling in their midst, the Exodus writer used the literary device of detailed repetition.

Second, in devoting one-fourth of the Exodus story to the Tabernacle, the writer may well have been emphasizing the importance of the Tabernacle and its use in worship not only to the people camped at the foot of the mountain but to all generations of their descendants for the next fifteen hundred years, as well as to Christian believers of all time whose spiritual roots extend back to the camp at the foot of the mountain.

The Sabbath

Before taking the first steps to bring the Tabernacle into reality, Moses reminds his people of their earlier instruction (31:12–17) that even as important as their present task is, they are not to work on the Sabbath (35:1–3). To make absolutely certain they understand, Moses repeats the instructions, "Six days shall work be done, but on the seventh day there shall be to you an holy day, a sabbath of rest to the Lord" (35:2). And then came a supplement not mentioned earlier—the prohibition against working included even the building of a fire (35:3).

The point is made. Nothing was to interfere with

their keeping of a day of worship for the Lord—not even something as important as the building of the place where He would dwell among them. The divine rhythm of one day set aside for the Lord was not to be broken.

It seems to me this particular instruction has a very practical application for us. We, too, need the rhythm of work and worship. And yet it becomes easy for people to get so busy doing good—even the work of the church—that we lose sight of the importance of rest, spiritual reflection, and worship. So often we find ourselves in danger of being so busy "building our tabernacles" that we actually neglect worship and praise. The result is lack of growth and spiritual poverty.

Offerings for the Lord

Again the people are told what kind of materials are needed for the building of the Tabernacle and its use as the house of the Lord, and they are urged to make offerings of them (35:4–29). First, the instructions given earlier (25:1–9) are repeated—gold, silver, brass, and acacia wood would be needed. They would also need the wide assortment of materials specified for the coverings and dividers; oil, spices, precious stones, cloth for the priests' clothing; materials for the building of the high fence that surrounded the courtyard are specified as were those materials needed for the building of the inside furnishings and the outside Altar and Laver (35:4–19).

Next we read that after hearing these instructions from Moses "all the congregation of the children of Israel departed from the presence of Moses. And they came, *every one whose heart stirred him up, and every one whom his spirit made willing,* and they brought the Lord's offering to the work of the tabernacle of the congregation, and for all his service, and for the holy garments" (35:20–21, italics mine). In verses 22 through 29 we're given the more specific details. Men and women willingly gave out of the resources collected just before leaving Egypt all that was necessary for building the Tabernacle complex.

Leaders to Direct the Work

Now we have the reaffirmation (see 31:1–111) of the two skilled craftsmen who were to be responsible for everything that was to be done in the building of the Tabernacle (35:30–36:7)—Bezaleel and Aholiab. These two gifted men were to direct all of the other skilled workers involved in the project. It was to them the people of Israel took all of the materials needed for the building, the furnishings, and the priests' clothing.

When all of the donated materials were amassed in one place, they made an intriguing discovery—not only had the people given enough for the entire project, they had given "more than enough." In fact, Moses had to tell them to stop giving. "Let neither man nor woman make any more work for the offering of the sanctuary. . . . For the stuff they had was sufficient for all the work to make it, *and too much*" (36:5–7, italics mine).

I have never heard of a twentieth-century pastor who had to tell the congregation to stop giving because the church had more than was needed!

The Building Itself

With all of the materials collected, the actual assembling of the building could now begin. First, all of the curtains and coverings were made for the tent part of the structure (36:8–19). See our discussion of these in Lesson 5 (26:1–14). Then the framework or the wooden structure itself was made (36:20–34). Again, in this part of our Scripture lesson, we find the detail noteworthy, even as we did when the instructions were first given by the Lord to Moses (26:15–30). Finally, the veil was assembled that divided the Holy of Holies from the Holy Place, as was the screen that was used for the door (36:35–38). For comparison read the description and our discussion in Lesson 5 (26:31–37).

Furnishings for the Holy of Holies and the Holy Place

With the completion of the basic structure, the craftsmen turned their attention to making the furnishings for the inside of the Tabernacle. First, came the Ark of the Covenant (37:1–9). As you will recall (25:10–22), the Ark was the only piece of furniture in the Holy of Holies and was to be positioned at the back or west wall. This magnificent gold plated chest was the repository for the tablets of the Law. And its lid with its gold cherubim's outstretched wings was called the mercy seat. There God said, "I will meet with thee, and I will commune with thee" (25:22).

The workers then made the table of acacia wood that was known as the Table of Shewbread (37:10–16). This is described in detail here even as it was in Lesson 5 (25:23–30). This table was to be placed along the north wall of the Tabernacle and in the Holy Place. Next came the Lampstand (37:17–24) which was to be positioned along the south wall of the Holy Place, right across from the Table. And, finally, the Altar of Incense was constructed (37:25–28) and would be placed next to the veil that divided the Holy Place from the Holy of Holies. A description of the Lampstand (25:31–40) and the Altar of Incense (30:1–10) is given in detail in Lesson 5. The making of the incense and the anointing oil is mentioned only briefly here (37:29), however, this was described in detail in our discussion of Chapter 30:22–38.

Furnishings in the Tabernacle Court

The large Altar where the animal sacrifices were offered was made next (38:1–7). The Altar was known as the Brazen Altar or the Brass Altar or the Altar of Holocaust. Its description in our Scripture lesson here matches the one we studied in Chapter 27:1–8. This Altar would be located inside the east gate in the Tabernacle court.

The Brass Laver, used for washing by the priests, was located between the Brazen Altar and the Tabernacle. This final bit of workmanship on the furnishings is accomplished (38:8). The Laver and its function was described in detail earlier (30:17–21), however, an interesting feature is added here—it was fashioned from the brass "lookingglasses of the women."

The Tabernacle Court

The final step in the process was the assembling of the hangings and the pillars that would form the "fence" that enclosed the Court (38:9–20). This, too, was described in detail in Lesson 5 and in Chapter 27:9–19.

An Inventory of Materials in the Tabernacle

Before closing out the description of the assembling of the Tabernacle, its coverings and furnishings, and the surrounding court, the Exodus writer gives us a summary of the materials donated by the people and how they were used (38:21–31). Again, the importance of this whole procedure is highlighted by the careful detail given in the Scripture lesson.

The Garments or Vestments for the Priests

The next step in the fulfilling of Moses' earlier instructions was the making and assembling of the clothing to be worn by the high priest and the priests (39:1). First, they made the Ephod (39:2–7)—also described in Chapter 28:6–12, Lesson 5; then, the Breastplate was made (39:8–21). This you recall was worn by the high priest and was also described in Chapter 28:13–30, Lesson 5. Then the artisans made the Robe of the Ephod (39:22–26), also worn by the high priest and described also in Chapter 28:31–35, Lesson 5. And, finally, all of the garments were made for the regular priests, Aaron's sons (39:27–31). These, too, were described earlier in Chapter 28:36–43, Lesson 5.

The Presentation to Moses of the Tabernacle

When everything had been built, woven, and assembled for the Tabernacle there was a grand presentation ceremony at which the people brought all of the parts to Moses (39:33–43). The Exodus writer then makes this grand statement, "According to all that the Lord commanded Moses, *so the children of Israel made all the work.* And Moses did look upon all the work, and, behold, they had done it as the Lord had commanded, even so had they done it: *and Moses blessed them*" (39:42–43, italics mine). What a justifiably proud day that must have been for all of them and especially for Moses. This stubborn (stiffnecked) group of people had not only freely given every bit of the material used, but they had also given of themselves in the building of everything that would be a part of and used in the Lord's house.

Once again, the Lord spoke to Moses and gave him instructions on assembling and putting together the framework structure (40:1–15). Step by step, the coverings were put on, the veils hung, and the furnishings were all placed exactly where the Lord had indicated. The poles and the hangings were installed that formed the fence around the Court of the Tabernacle, and the gate was put in place. Then the Brazen Altar and the Laver were installed in their proper places inside the court.

At each step in this building process the work was consecrated. And when everything was finished—the tables of Law were in the Ark, bread was arranged properly on the table, the lamps in the candlestick were lit, and the incense was burning—Moses offered a sacrifice on the Altar. It was then the Exodus writer tells us that "Moses finished the work" (40:33).

The Tabernacle was completed on the first anniversary of the Exodus from Egypt. It was ready now for the presence of the Lord. "Then a cloud covered the tent of the congregation, and the glory of the Lord filled the tabernacle" (40:34).

Now that God's dwelling place was set in the middle of the camp and a place of worship was firmly established, the Hebrews were ready to move on. But they would move only under the guidance of God. As in the past, God continued to supply direction for His people through the movement of the cloud. "And when the cloud was taken up from over the tabernacle, the children of Israel went onward in all their journeys: But if the cloud were not taken up, then they journeyed not till the day that it was taken up" (40:36–37).

As Christians who have put our faith in God, we all long to know that God is guiding us. We don't want to wander through life haphazardly. Above all else we want to feel secure and know that we're heading in the right direction—the way God wants us to go.

The Tabernacle Is Erected and Dedicated

A Modern Parable of God's Leading

171

I remember stumbling out of the woods in the dark one summer night after spending the day hunting. Foolishly, I had waited too long to head back to my car, and it was pitch dark as I emerged from the forest.

As I stood on the border between the tall pines and the plowed fields, I couldn't see a thing, let alone my car that was parked somewhere in the distance. I remembered I had to cross two plowed fields and pick my way through several barbed wire fences. But I couldn't see my hand in front of my face.

While I was leaning against a tree trying to figure out what to do, I heard the distant thunder of a summer storm. It wasn't long before the thunder sounded closer indicating the storm was moving in my direction. Heat lightning began to flash periodically and illumine the sky. During one brilliant explosion of light, I caught a glimpse of my car off to the right a half mile or so. Then it was black again.

Slowly I began to inch my way along like a blind man in the direction of the car. But after going a little ways I became unsure of myself and waited for the lightning to flash again. When it did, I could see far enough to go a little further with confidence. Then I would wait for another lightning flash. Finally, with a great surge of relief I made it to the car and then was on my way safely home.

So often in life when I've been in need of God's direction but have been stumbling around in the darkness of my ignorance and confusion I've remembered that dark night. Then I've remembered, too, that God always provides us with enough light for the next little ways in life's journey. Fitfully, we'd like to have a plan of action for the whole trip, but God doesn't necessarily respond that way. But of one thing we can be sure—if we trust Him, He'll light up as much of the way as we need for the moment.

The Good News that shines brightly in the Book of Exodus is that our God is faithful to lead His people. If we look for His leadership, we'll find it. We may not see a visible cloud in our sky in daytime and we may not see a pillar of fire moving before us at night, but God will break into our awareness and lead us safely forward. We can count on Him for direction.

For what may seem like "forty days and forty nights" we have been on a journey of faith together with the Hebrew people as they moved out of Egyptian slavery into the vast Sinai peninsula and east to the mountain itself. And there we've camped with them at the foot of the mountain of God. There is much that has been strange as we've tried to understand and capture the thinking of this ancient people. At times we may have wondered: What does this mean to me? This is especially true as we've learned about the Tabernacle—the portable dwelling place of God among His people and the strange rituals which accompanied their worship.

But it is useful for us as Christians to get an understanding of the practices and faith of our Hebrew spiritual ancestors. This helps us understand better not only our studies in the Old Testament but those in the New Testament as well. At the same time familiarity with the Hebrew understanding of God and the focus and meaning of their worship can enrich our own experience of faith.

The message of our Exodus story is that God wants to be at the center of our lives in the divine rhythm of work and worship. While we may not always "feel" His presence, we can be certain that He is with us. We have learned, too, that the God of the Exodus drama amply provides for the needs of His people— leadership, freedom, welfare, laws, worship, forgiveness, His presence, and His guidance.

The message of the Exodus story is rich in the drama of God's covenant with His people—a covenant made with Abraham, ratified with the later Patriarchs and affirmed again at Sinai. It was this relationship between God and His people that remained in effect for more than fifteen hundred years. Then, as we comprehend the meaning of that relationship, we can better understand the new covenant that had its beginnings with the birth of Jesus and became a reality with His death and resurrection and the coming of the Spirit at Pentecost.

With rich imagery and color, the writer of the

Lessons for Today's Christian

Book of the Hebrews in looking back over the events we've just studied captured the difference between the old and the new, "But Christ being come an high priest of good things to come, by a greater and more perfect tabernacle, not made with hands, that is to say not of this building; Neither by the blood of goats and calves, but by his own blood he entered in once into the holy place, having obtained eternal redemption for us" (Heb. 9:11–12).

Without minimizing the meaning of the Tabernacle and the Old Testament rituals of worship for the people of God under the old covenant, the writer of Hebrews ends a powerful chapter with this grand conclusion, "So Christ was once offered to bear the sins of many; and unto them that look for him shall he appear the second time without sin unto salvation" (9:28).

Lord God, Just to know that I was created to have You at the center of my life helps to satisfy my deepest longing. Thank You for being my center, my fullness, my motivation for living. Amen.

WHAT THIS SCRIPTURE MEANS TO ME
Exodus 35—40

As I read this Scripture lesson, I wished that God's blueprints for our individual lives were as clear as His detailed instructions for the building of the tabernacle. If they were, we would know exactly what God expected us to do in every situation. But things aren't quite that simple. Our days are filled with situations in which we must struggle to discern the instructions we are to obey. At the same time, like the children of Israel, our obedience is required.

In his moving poem, "Obedience," Stanley Wiersma recalls a childhood scene that had burned into his memory. One Sunday morning his father read the weather report in the sky: a storm was on its way. That in itself was little cause for alarm except that he had not yet mowed a large, perfectly ripe field of oats.

Stanley's father knew the storm was a few hours off; if the family pulled together and worked hard, they could save most of the harvest. But they didn't. Following the father's example, everyone dressed for church and, once there, heartily sang psalm after psalm of praise. While the congregation worshiped, wind, rain, and hail flattened the field. After church the family went to assess the severe crop damage. Young Stanley noticed that his father expressed no regrets for having been loyal to his convictions regarding a Sabbath respite from work. That day the older generation, by actions rather than by words, taught the younger what obedience was all about: standing firm "according to all that the Lord had commanded" (36:1).

As a grown man, Stanley's own conscience was sensitive to issues other than such strict Sabbath observance, yet he was careful to listen for God's voice and to follow the instructions he heard.

One thing I do know about God's blueprint for my life and work: it is uniquely mine, and it is built on a foundation of talents that God has given me. According to their individual talents and resources, the children of Israel constructed the tabernacle and wove the priests' garments. God required that these special talents be used for His glory.

My sister recently told me about her tenant who, although she is mentally impaired, is able to live alone and take care of herself. She has found a church home where she faithfully completes a small task that contributes to the smooth functioning of the community: Every Sunday morning she goes to church early so she can fold the service bulletins before they are distributed by the ushers. This woman's work may be equivalent to just one piece in a giant one-thousand-piece jigsaw puzzle, but without it, the picture could not be whole.

In Matthew 25 Jesus tells a story of a man who was severely judged for burying in the ground a gold piece entrusted to him, in order to keep it safe, rather than risk it in trade in order to add to it. That story is often called the parable of the talents. It reinforces what I read in this Old Testament story of the building of the Tabernacle: we're called to obey God's blueprint and that includes investing our talents and resources in God's work.